PEACOCK PANTRY

Favorite Recipes from Peacock Hill Country Inn

PEACOCK PANTRY

Favorite Recipes from Peacock Hill Country Inn

Published by Anita Rodgers Ogilvie

Library of Congress Control Number: 2002105427
ISBN: 0-9720128-0-X

Edited, Designed, and Manufactured by
Favorite Recipes® Press
An imprint of

FRP

P. O. Box 305142
Nashville, Tennessee 37230
800-358-0560

Art Director: Steve Newman
Book Design: Starletta Polster
Project Editor: Linda Jones

Manufactured in the United States of America
First Printing: 2002
6,000 copies

The *Peacock Pantry* is blessed—

Many times been put to the test.

Our children requested first

That these recipes, even the worst,

Be put into print.

Guests have come and gone—

Each unique, many asking timidly or boldly,

"Would you...? Could you...? Give me...??"

"That recipe"..."Thought you would never ask!"

"My pleasure"...and...Thank you

For making the many hours seem few.

God only knows how much we love

And enjoy serving each and every one of you!

Please use this cookbook.

Make notes and corrections in it.

Enjoy each recipe and may you find

Satisfaction and confidence in each recipe you prepare.

Contents

Contents

History of Peacock Hill Country Inn

The history of Peacock Hill Country Inn actually began in the
1853-1857 pre-Civil War period when the main building of
the inn, now called the Farmhouse, was built.

During the Civil War, the house was spared from being
burned down by Yankee raiding parties due to the influence of
the builder, who was a Northern sympathizer. Since that time,
six generations of folks have lived in the house and called this
Flat Creek community of College Grove, Tennessee, their home.

In 1992, the farm was purchased by Walter and Anita Ogilvie
with renovation of the farmhouse beginning the following year.
The front three rooms and the front porch of the original house
were retained. The hand hewed red cedar beams,
partially displayed in the walls and ceilings, and the two large
rock fireplaces, are the highlights of these rooms.

The rest of the farmhouse was built in 1993-94 with the
objective of blending the "old" with the convenience of the "new."
(See the book cover for a picture of the farmhouse.)

Today, Peacock Hill is a luxury country inn consisting of
several buildings on a one-thousand-acre retreat with
eight years' experience of serving guests delicious breakfasts,
lunches, suppers, and candlelight dinners. This cookbook
shares those experiences with you.

Rock fences built by slaves on the Farm.

Appetizers and Beverages

You make the grass

for cattle and vegetables

for the people.

You make food grow

from the earth.

You give us wine

that makes happy hearts

and olive oil that

makes our faces shine.

You give us bread that

gives us strength.

Psalm 104:14-15
New Century Version

Antipasto Platter

This pretty presentation just happens to be delicious, too.

1 small head cauliflower
8 ounces green beans, trimmed
8 ounces whole mushrooms
2 red bell peppers, cut into strips
Italian salad dressing
Romaine or leaf lettuce
3 ounces dry salami, sliced
3 ounces pepperoni, sliced
1 cup cooked fresh tuna
4 ounces provolone cheese,
   thinly sliced, rolled up
4 ounces mozzarella cheese,
   thinly sliced, rolled up
4 ounces goat cheese, cut into
   1/2-inch cubes (optional)

- Steam the cauliflower in a steamer for 7 minutes. Rinse under cold water and drain. Steam the green beans in a steamer for 6 minutes. Rinse under cold water and drain.

- Place the cauliflower, green beans, mushrooms and bell peppers in separate bowls. Pour Italian salad dressing over the vegetables. Marinate, covered, in the refrigerator for several hours.

- Line a large platter with lettuce. Drain the vegetables, discarding the marinade. Arrange the vegetables in groups on the lettuce. Continue to arrange the salami, pepperoni, tuna, provolone cheese, mozzarella cheese and goat cheese on the lettuce.

Serves 8 to 10

Other Additions:
Add one 15-ounce can garbanzo beans, drained, rinsed and
   marinated in Italian salad dressing.
Add one 15-ounce jar marinated artichokes, drained.
Add 2 hard-cooked eggs, cut into wedges.
Add 1 cup drained black olives.
Add 1 bunch green onions.
Add 2 tablespoons well-drained capers.
Add other favorite cheeses.

Cheese Pennies

These disappear quickly, so prepare many.

1/2 cup (1 stick) unsalted butter,
  softened
8 ounces sharp Cheddar cheese,
  grated (2 cups)
1 1/2 cups flour
1/2 teaspoon salt
1/2 to 1 teaspoon cayenne pepper

- Cream the butter in a mixing bowl until light and fluffy. Add the cheese and mix well. Add the flour, salt and cayenne pepper gradually, stirring well after each addition. The dough will be stiff.

- Shape the dough into two 9-inch logs, 1 inch in diameter. Wrap in waxed paper and then in foil. Chill for 8 to 12 hours.

- Preheat the oven to 375 degrees.

- Cut the logs into slices 1/8 to 1/4 inch thick. Arrange on an ungreased baking sheet.

- Bake for 12 minutes.

- Store in an airtight container.

Makes 2 to 3 dozen

Corn Rounds

Yummy.

4 ears fresh corn
1/4 cup (1/2 stick) butter
1 tablespoon chopped fresh
  oregano leaves
1/2 teaspoon cumin
1/4 teaspoon salt
1/4 teaspoon cayenne pepper

- Shuck the corn and remove the silk. Rinse and pat dry. Cut the corn into 1 1/2-inch rounds.

- Boil the corn in water to cover in a large saucepan for 3 to 4 minutes or until tender; drain.

- Melt the butter with the oregano, cumin, salt and cayenne pepper in a large skillet. Add the corn and toss to coat.

- Cook for 2 to 3 minutes or until heated through. Serve hot.

Serves 4 to 6

Cinnamon Pecans

1 egg white
1 tablespoon cold water
1/2 cup sugar
1/2 teaspoon cinnamon
1/4 teaspoon salt
3 cups pecan halves

- Preheat the oven to 225 degrees.

- Beat the egg white and cold water in a mixing bowl until foamy. Add the sugar, cinnamon and salt gradually, beating until stiff peaks form.

- Add the pecans and stir to coat. Spread on a baking sheet sprayed with nonstick cooking spray.

- Bake for 45 minutes or until the pecans are dry and brown, stirring frequently.

Serves 6

Guacamole

3 avocados, coarsely mashed
1 tablespoon lemon juice
1 teaspoon Worcestershire sauce
2 medium tomatoes, peeled,
    seeded, chopped
1 teaspoon salt
1/8 teaspoon hot sauce
1 garlic clove, crushed

- Combine the avocados, lemon juice and Worcestershire sauce in a bowl and mix well. Add the tomatoes, salt, hot sauce and garlic and mix well.

- Spoon into a serving dish. Chill, covered, until ready to serve.

- Serve with corn chips or as part of a salad with shredded lettuce.

Serves 8

Herbed Bread Thins

Nice to serve with soups, dips, etc. Enjoy!

1 garlic clove, crushed
1/2 cup (1 stick) butter, softened
1 teaspoon basil
1/2 teaspoon tarragon
1/2 teaspoon chervil
1 teaspoon chopped fresh parsley
1 (2-inch-diameter) loaf French
    bread, cut into thin slices

- Blend the garlic, butter, basil, tarragon, chervil and parsley in a blender until smooth. Spoon into a small bowl. Chill, covered, for 8 to 12 hours.

- Preheat the oven to 325 degrees.

- Bring the garlic mixture to room temperature. Brush over the bread slices. Arrange the slices on a baking sheet.

- Bake until brown.

Serves 8

Crostini

1/3 cup olive oil
1 tablespoon minced garlic
2 tablespoons chopped fresh
    parsley
2 loaves French bread, cut into
    1/2-inch slices
Cheese Topping or Tomato
    Topping (below)

- Preheat the oven to 350 degrees.

- Combine the olive oil and garlic in a small bowl and mix well. Stir in the parsley.

- Brush 1 side of each bread slice with the garlic mixture. Arrange brushed side up on a baking sheet.

- Bake for 6 to 8 minutes.

- Top with the Cheese Topping or Tomato Topping.

Serves 16

Cheese Topping

16 ounces mozzarella cheese,
    cut into 1-inch pieces
1 teaspoon olive oil
1/2 teaspoon chopped fresh basil

- Combine the mozzarella cheese, olive oil and basil in a bowl and toss to mix well.

- Chill, covered, for up to 2 days.

Tomato Topping

1 pint cherry or grape tomatoes,
    cut into quarters
1 tablespoon olive oil
1 teaspoon chopped fresh basil
1/2 teaspoon lemon juice
1/2 teaspoon salt
1/2 teaspoon freshly ground pepper

- Combine the tomatoes, olive oil, basil, lemon juice, salt and pepper in a bowl and toss to mix well.

- Chill, covered, for up to 1 day.

Pesto and Cheese Hors d'Oeuvres

3 ounces cream cheese, softened
2 garlic cloves, minced
1 loaf French bread, split
    lengthwise
1/2 cup Basil Pesto (below)
2 tomatoes, seeded, chopped,
    drained
Freshly grated Parmesan cheese

- Preheat the oven to 350 degrees.

- Combine the cream cheese and garlic in a bowl and mix well. Spread on the cut side of the bread. Spread Basil Pesto over the cream cheese mixture. Sprinkle with the tomatoes and Parmesan cheese.

- Arrange on a baking sheet. Bake for 10 minutes or until the cheese is melted.

- Cut into serving pieces and serve immediately.

Serves 8

Basil Pesto

2 cups firmly packed fresh basil
    leaves
2 sprigs of fresh parsley
2 garlic cloves, minced
3 tablespoons pine nuts
1/4 cup freshly grated Parmesan
    cheese
1/4 teaspoon salt
Pepper to taste
3 tablespoons olive oil

- Combine the basil, parsley, garlic, pine nuts, Parmesan cheese, salt and pepper in a blender. Add the olive oil in a fine stream, processing constantly.

- Spoon into a bowl. Chill, covered, until ready to use.

- Note: Bring to room temperature before tossing with fresh cooked pasta.

Makes 1/2 cup

Herbed Cheese-Stuffed Mushrooms

12 ounces large fresh mushrooms
3 ounces cream cheese, softened
1/2 cup freshly grated Parmesan
    cheese
1 1/2 teaspoons chopped fresh
    rosemary
1/4 teaspoon Worcestershire sauce
1 tablespoon chopped fresh parsley
1 1/2 teaspoons chopped fresh thyme
Pinch of salt, pepper and nutmeg

- Preheat the oven to 350 degrees.

- Remove the stems from the mushrooms. Peel the mushroom caps.

- Combine the cream cheese, Parmesan cheese, rosemary, Worcestershire sauce, parsley, thyme, salt, pepper and nutmeg in a small bowl and mix well.

- Spoon into the mushroom caps. Arrange in a lightly greased 9×13-inch baking pan.

- Bake for 20 minutes.

Serves 8 or makes about 1 1/2 dozen

Léa, one of my dearest innkeepers from France, taught me how to "peel" mushrooms. She learned from her mother. Peeling the mushrooms keeps them from feeling "slimy" (no washing) and is so clean. Just take a small paring knife and tuck the blade at the edge of the mushroom. Grasp the outer layer with your thumb and pull towards you. Very easy and looks so neat.

Berry Hot Cider

Very pretty and so good.

8 cups apple cider
1 (10-ounce) package
   unsweetened red raspberries
1 (4-inch) cinnamon stick
1 1/2 teaspoons whole cloves
Apple wedges

- Combine the apple cider, raspberries, cinnamon and cloves in a saucepan and mix well. Bring to a boil and reduce the heat. Simmer for 10 minutes. Strain through a cheesecloth-lined strainer into a pitcher, discarding the solids.

- Pour into serving cups. Float an apple wedge in each cup.

Serves 6 to 8

Hot Cranberry Apple Punch

2 cups boiling water
8 Cranberry Cove tea bags
4 cups apple juice or apple cider
Orange slices

- Pour boiling water over the tea bags in a large saucepan. Steep for 5 minutes. Discard the tea bags. Stir in the apple juice.

- Heat to serving temperature. Do not boil.

- Ladle into serving cups. Float an orange slice in each cup.

Serves 6 to 8

Hot Spiced Apple Juice

Nice to serve on a cold winter afternoon.

2 (12-ounce) cans frozen
   unsweetened apple juice
   concentrate, thawed
4 cups water
2 cups fresh cranberries
2 (3-inch) sticks cinnamon
6 whole cloves

- Combine the apple juice concentrate and water in a large saucepan. Add the cranberries, cinnamon sticks and cloves.

- Bring to a boil and reduce the heat. Simmer, covered, for 30 minutes.

- Strain the mixture, discarding the cranberries and spices.

- Ladle into serving cups.

Makes 1/2 gallon

Instant Cappuccino Mix

1 (8-ounce) jar instant decaffeinated or regular coffee
1 (14-quart) package instant dry milk powder
1 (16-ounce) jar dry nondairy creamer
1 (2-pound) container chocolate drink mix
1 (1-pound) package confectioners' sugar

- Combine the coffee granules, dry milk powder, nondairy creamer, chocolate drink mix and confectioners' sugar in a large bowl and mix well.

- Store in airtight containers in a cool place.

- To serve, combine 2 to 3 tablespoons of the mixture with 1 cup hot water in a cup or mug and stir until dissolved.

Makes about 12 cups mix

Instant Cocoa Mix

A favorite with many and our family, too.

2³/4 cups instant nonfat dry milk powder
1¹/2 cups chocolate drink mix
¹/2 cup dry nondairy creamer
¹/2 cup confectioners' sugar
1 cup miniature marshmallows (optional)

- Combine the dry milk powder, chocolate drink mix, nondairy creamer, confectioners' sugar and marshmallows in a large bowl and mix well.

- Store in an airtight container.

- To serve, combine ¹/3 cup of the mixture with 1 cup boiling water in a cup or mug and stir until dissolved.

Makes 5 cups mix

Spiced Hot Chocolate Mix

5¹/2 cups instant dry milk powder
2¹/2 cups chocolate drink mix
2 cups miniature marshmallows (optional)
³/4 cup dry nondairy creamer
3 tablespoons cinnamon

- Combine the dry milk powder, chocolate drink mix, marshmallows, nondairy creamer and cinnamon in a large bowl and mix well.

- Store in an airtight container.

- To serve, combine ¹/3 cup of the mixture with ³/4 cup boiling water in a cup or mug and stir until dissolved.

Makes 8¹/2 cups mix

Half-and-Half Drink

3 cups cranberry juice
3 cups unsweetened pineapple
    juice

- Combine the cranberry juice and pineapple juice in a large pitcher and mix well.

- Chill, covered, until ready to serve.

- Serve over ice cubes.

- Note: Try other juice combinations such as cranberry juice and orange juice; orange juice and pineapple juice; apple juice and pineapple juice, etc. Always use unsweetened juices when available.

Serves 6

Blackberry Lemonade

A winner for hot summer days.

3½ pints fresh blackberries
2 (12-ounce) cans frozen
    lemonade concentrate,
    thawed
12 cups water
3 tablespoons sugar

- Purée the blackberries in a blender or food processor. Strain into a pitcher, discarding the solids.

- Add the lemonade concentrate, water and sugar and mix well.

- Chill, covered, until ready to serve.

- Serve over ice cubes and garnish with lemon slices and fresh mint.

Serves 12

Sunny Lemonade

Superb.

6 cups white grape juice, chilled
1 (12-ounce) can frozen
 lemonade concentrate,
 thawed
5 1/2 cups club soda, chilled

- Combine the white grape juice, lemonade concentrate and club soda in a 1-gallon container and stir to mix well.

- Serve over ice.

Makes 3 quarts

Just Plain Lemonade

1 1/4 cups fresh lemon juice
3/4 cup sugar
4 1/4 cups cold water
Lemon slices

- Combine the lemon juice and sugar in a large pitcher and stir until the sugar dissolves.

- Add the water and lemon slices and stir to mix well.

- Chill, covered, until ready to serve.

- Serve over ice cubes and garnish with lemon slices.

Makes 1 1/2 quarts

Make decorative ice cubes

by placing a twist of lemon

inside each ice cube space

and add water to cover.

Freeze until firm.

The Fuzzy Peach Drink

A refreshing summertime drink.

1 or 2 fresh peaches
1 (6-ounce) can frozen lemonade
   concentrate

- Cut the unpeeled peaches into halves and remove the pits.

- Combine the peaches and lemonade concentrate in a blender. Add enough ice cubes to fill the remaining space. Process until blended.

Serves 3 or 4

Pineapple Yogurt Smoothie

Delicious.

3/4 cup frozen unsweetened
   pineapple juice concentrate,
   thawed
1 cup vanilla yogurt
1/2 cup skim milk
1/2 cup water
2 tablespoons sugar
1 1/2 teaspoons vanilla extract
Ice cubes

- Process the pineapple juice concentrate, yogurt, milk, water, sugar and vanilla in a blender until smooth.

- Add enough ice cubes to fill to the 5-cup level. Process until frothy.

Makes 5 servings

*He who spends time on his knees
has no trouble standing on his feet.*

Strawberry Slush

Delightfully simple, yet delicious.

2 cups fresh strawberries
12 ice cubes
1 (6-ounce) can frozen orange
    juice concentrate
1 tablespoon sugar, or to taste
White wine to taste (optional)

- Rinse the strawberries and remove the caps.

- Process the ice cubes in a blender until crushed. Add the strawberries, orange juice concentrate, sugar and white wine. Process until a slushy consistency.

- Pour into chilled wineglasses. Garnish each serving with a fresh strawberry.

Serves 3 or 4

Cranberry Shrub

A nice color and makes a great punch, too.

1 (46-ounce) bottle cranberry
    juice cocktail, chilled
1 (46-ounce) bottle pineapple
    juice, chilled
Lemon sherbet

- Combine the cranberry juice cocktail and pineapple juice in a pitcher and stir to blend well.

- Pour into glasses and add a scoop of lemon sherbet.

- Serve immediately.

- For punch, add 1 quart lemon-lime soda for every gallon of shrub.

Serves 10 to 12

Breads

God said,

Look, I have given

you all the plants

that have grain for seeds

and all the trees

whose fruits have seeds

in them. They

will be food for you.

Genesis 1:29
New Century Version

Cinnamon Potato Rolls

The popular cinnamon rolls that are served at the inn every week.

2 envelopes dry yeast
1 1/2 cups warm water
3/4 cup sugar
3/4 cup hot mashed cooked potatoes
1 1/3 cups packed brown sugar
1/2 teaspoon cinnamon
3 tablespoons cream
2 tablespoons butter, softened
2 eggs
1/2 cup (1 stick) butter, softened
2 teaspoons salt
6 1/2 cups flour
Confectioners' sugar icing
    (optional)

- Dissolve the yeast in the warm water in a small bowl. Combine the sugar and mashed potatoes in a large mixing bowl. Add the yeast mixture and mix well. Let rise, tightly covered, in a warm place for 1 hour or until doubled in bulk.

- Combine the brown sugar, cinnamon, cream and 2 tablespoons butter in a bowl and mix well.

- Stir the dough down. Add the eggs, 1/2 cup butter and salt and mix well. Stir in the flour gradually. Knead on a lightly floured surface until smooth and elastic. Divide the dough into 2 equal portions. Roll each portion into a 12-inch square. Spread the brown sugar mixture over each square to within 1 inch of the edges. Roll up as for a jelly roll. Cut each roll into slices. Arrange in a greased baking pan. Let rise, covered, in a warm place for 1 hour or until doubled in bulk.

- Preheat the oven to 350 degrees.

- Bake for 25 to 30 minutes or until golden brown. Watch carefully to prevent overbrowning.

- Drizzle with confectioners' sugar icing, if desired. To make the icing, combine confectioners' sugar and vanilla extract to taste in a bowl. Stir in enough boiling water gradually to make the desired consistency.

- Note: Use dental floss to cut through the dough. Just place the floss under the dough and bring it up and cross, using both hands. When the floss crosses it will cut the dough.

Makes 1 dozen

Buttermilk Oat Rolls

3/4 cup rolled oats
1/2 cup boiling water
1 tablespoon sugar
1 envelope dry yeast
1 1/2 teaspoons sugar
1/4 cup warm water
2 1/4 cups flour
1/4 cup buttermilk
1 tablespoon butter, melted
3/4 teaspoon salt

- Mix the oats, 1/2 cup boiling water and 1 tablespoon sugar in a small bowl. Let stand for 5 minutes.

- Dissolve the yeast and 1 1/2 teaspoons sugar in 1/4 cup warm water in a large bowl. Let stand for 5 minutes. Add the oat mixture, 1 3/4 cups of the flour, the buttermilk, butter and salt and mix well.

- Knead on a lightly floured surface until smooth and elastic, adding enough of the remaining flour to prevent the dough from sticking to your hands. Place in a large bowl coated with nonstick cooking spray, turning to coat the surface.

- Let rise, covered, in a warm place for 45 minutes or until doubled in bulk. Punch the dough down. Cover and let rest for 5 minutes.

- Divide the dough into 12 equal portions. Shape each portion into a ball. Arrange in a baking pan coated with nonstick cooking spray. Cover and let rise for 30 minutes or until doubled in bulk.

- Preheat the oven to 375 degrees.

- Uncover the rolls. Bake for 25 minutes or until light brown.

- Note: You may brush a mixture of 1 egg white and 1 tablespoon water over the rolls and sprinkle with 1 tablespoon rolled oats before baking.

Makes 1 dozen

French Rolls or Buns

Another regular standby at Peacock Hill.

3 1/4 to 4 1/4 cups flour
2 tablespoons sugar
1 1/2 teaspoons salt
2 envelopes dry yeast
2 tablespoons butter, softened
1 1/2 cups warm water
Cornmeal

- Sift 1 1/2 cups flour, sugar, salt and yeast into a large mixing bowl. Add the butter. Stir in the warm water gradually. Beat for 2 minutes, scraping the side of the bowl occasionally. Add 1/2 cup of the remaining flour. Beat at high speed for 2 minutes, scraping the side of the bowl. Stir in enough of the remaining flour to make a soft dough.

- Knead on a lightly floured surface a few times. Shape into a ball. Place in a greased bowl, turning to coat the surface. Cover the bowl tightly. Chill for 2 hours or up to 2 days.

- Punch the dough down. Divide into 24 equal portions. Shape each portion into a smooth egg shape. Arrange on greased baking sheets sprinkled with cornmeal. Cover and let rise in a warm place for 1 hour or until doubled in bulk. Cut a slash in the top of each roll with a sharp knife.

- Preheat the oven to 400 degrees.

- Bake for 10 minutes or until golden brown.

- Note: These rolls freeze beautifully. Remove the rolls from the oven when they are cooked through, but just before they turn brown. Cool completely. Place in freezer bags and store in the freezer.

Makes 1 1/2 to 2 dozen

Yogurt Crescent Rolls

These delicious rolls are great to serve for a ladies' luncheon.

1/3 cup vegetable oil
1 cup plain yogurt
1/2 cup sugar
4 cups flour
1 teaspoon salt
2 envelopes dry yeast
1/2 cup warm water
1 egg
1 egg white
Butter or vegetable oil for
  brushing

- Mix the oil, yogurt and sugar in a bowl. Mix the flour and salt together.

- Dissolve the yeast in the warm water in a large bowl. Let stand for 5 minutes. Add the yogurt mixture, egg and egg white. Add 2 cups of the flour mixture. Beat at medium speed until smooth. Stir in the remaining flour mixture gradually. Cover and chill for 8 to 12 hours.

- Punch the dough down. Divide into 4 equal portions. Roll each portion into a 10-inch circle. Brush with butter. Cut each circle into 12 wedges. Roll up and place on greased baking sheets. Cover and let rise for 45 minutes or until doubled in bulk.

- Preheat the oven to 375 degrees.

- Bake for 10 minutes or until golden brown.

Makes 4 dozen

Horse and buggy ride at Peacock Hill.

Beautiful Brown Rolls

Nan's favorite roll.

2 cups boiling water
1 cup quick-cooking oats
2 envelopes dry yeast
1/4 cup warm water
2 eggs, beaten
1/2 cup molasses
1/2 cup vegetable oil
1/3 cup sugar
1/2 teaspoon salt
5 3/4 to 6 1/4 cups flour
Melted butter

- Combine 2 cups boiling water and the oats in a large mixing bowl and mix well. Cool to lukewarm.

- Dissolve the yeast in 1/4 cup warm water in a small bowl. Stir into the oat mixture. Add the eggs, molasses, oil, sugar and salt and mix well. Stir in enough of the flour to form a soft dough.

- Knead on a lightly floured surface for 6 to 8 minutes or until smooth and elastic. Place in a greased bowl, turning to coat the surface. Cover and let rise in a warm place for 1 hour or until doubled in bulk.

- Punch the dough down. Divide into 36 equal portions. Shape each portion into a roll. Arrange on greased baking sheets. Cover and let rise for 30 minutes or until doubled in bulk.

- Preheat the oven to 375 degrees.

- Bake for 20 to 25 minutes or until golden brown. Brush with butter. Cool on wire racks.

Makes 3 dozen

If at first you don't succeed,
skydiving is not for you!

Potato Bread or Buns or Rolls

1 medium potato, peeled,
   cut into cubes
1 1/2 cups water
1 cup buttermilk
3 tablespoons sugar
2 tablespoons butter
2 teaspoons salt
6 to 6 1/2 cups flour
2 envelopes dry yeast

- Cook the potato in the water in a saucepan for 12 minutes or until tender. Do not drain. Mash the potato, adding additional water if needed to make 1 3/4 cups. Add the buttermilk, sugar, butter and salt and mix well. Cool to 120 to 130 degrees on a thermometer.

- Combine 2 cups of the flour and the yeast in a large mixing bowl. Add the potato mixture. Beat at low speed for 30 seconds. Beat at high speed for 3 minutes. Stir in as much of the remaining flour as possible.

- Knead on a lightly floured surface for 6 to 8 minutes or until smooth and elastic. Place in a greased bowl, turning to grease the surface. Cover and let rise for 1 hour.

- Punch the dough down. Divide into 2 equal portions. Divide each portion into 12 equal portions. Shape into balls. Dip the top of each ball in additional flour. Arrange on greased baking sheets. Cover and let rise for 30 minutes.

- Preheat the oven to 375 degrees.

- Bake for 20 to 25 minutes or until golden brown.

Makes 2 dozen

French Bread

An all-time standby at Peacock Hill.

1 envelope dry yeast
2 teaspoons salt
1 tablespoon sugar
2 cups warm water
5 1/2 to 6 cups unbleached flour
2 tablespoons (about) cornmeal
Butter for brushing

- Dissolve the yeast, salt and sugar in the warm water in a large bowl. Stir in enough flour gradually until the mixture refuses to absorb any more flour. Knead on a lightly floured surface for 5 minutes or until smooth and elastic. Shape into a ball. Place in a greased bowl, turning to coat the surface. Cover and let rise in a warm place for 1 hour or until doubled in bulk. Grease a baking sheet and sprinkle with the cornmeal.

- Punch down the dough. Divide into 2 equal portions. Shape each portion into a long narrow loaf. Arrange on the prepared baking sheet. Make several shallow diagonal cuts across the tops of the loaves with a sharp knife. Brush with butter so the top will be soft. Let rise for 30 to 40 minutes or until doubled in bulk.

- Preheat the oven to 450 degrees. Bake for 5 minutes. Reduce the oven temperature to 350 degrees. Bake for 10 minutes. Remove to wire racks to cool.

Makes 2 loaves

Honey Wheat Bread

A super bread for sandwiches or just to eat.

1/4 cup honey
2 envelopes dry yeast
2 cups warm water
1/4 cup honey
4 cups all-purpose flour
3 cups whole wheat flour
1 cup plain nonfat yogurt
1/4 cup plus 2 tablespoons
   vegetable oil
1 tablespoon salt
2 cups all-purpose flour,
   if needed

- Dissolve 1/4 cup honey and the yeast in the warm water in a large bowl. Let stand for 5 minutes. Add 1/4 cup honey, 4 cups all-purpose flour, the whole wheat flour, yogurt, oil and salt and mix well.

- Knead on a lightly floured surface until smooth and elastic, adding the remaining 2 cups all-purpose flour if needed. Cover and let rise in a warm place until doubled in bulk.

- Punch the dough down. Divide into 2 equal portions. Shape each portion into a loaf. Place in two greased 5×9-inch loaf pans. Cover and let rise until doubled in bulk.

- Preheat the oven to 350 degrees. Bake for 45 minutes or until the loaves sound hollow when tapped on the bottom. Remove the loaves from the pans and cool on wire racks.

Makes 2 loaves

Dill Bread

Makes a great ham sandwich.

1 envelope dry yeast
1/4 cup warm water
3 tablespoons minced onion
1 tablespoon butter
1 cup small-curd creamed
    cottage cheese
2 tablespoons sugar
2 teaspoons dillweed
1 teaspoon salt
1/4 teaspoon baking soda
1 egg
2 1/4 to 2 1/2 cups flour
Butter for brushing

- Dissolve the yeast in the warm water in a small bowl.

- Sauté the onion in 1 tablespoon butter in a small skillet until translucent.

- Heat the cottage cheese in a saucepan until lukewarm.

- Combine the yeast mixture, sautéed onion, cottage cheese, sugar, dillweed, salt, baking soda and egg in a large mixing bowl and mix well. Add enough of the flour gradually to form a dough that can be handled easily without sticking, stirring well after each addition.

- Knead on a lightly floured surface until smooth and elastic. Place in a greased bowl, turning to coat the surface. Cover and let rise in a warm place for 1 1/4 hours or until doubled in bulk.

- Punch the dough down. Shape into a loaf. Place in a well-greased 5×9-inch loaf pan. Let rise for 45 minutes or until the dough rises to just above the edge of the pan.

- Preheat the oven to 350 degrees.

- Bake for 35 to 45 minutes or until golden brown. Brush the top with butter.

Makes 1 loaf

31

Focaccia

1 envelope quick-rising yeast
1 cup lukewarm water
1/4 cup olive oil
2 tablespoons vegetable oil
1 tablespoon sugar
1/2 teaspoon salt
2 3/4 to 3 cups unbleached flour
1/4 cup cornmeal
1 medium garlic clove, minced
2 tablespoons vegetable oil
2 teaspoons crushed fresh
   rosemary, or 1 teaspoon
   dried rosemary
1 to 2 teaspoons kosher salt

- Dissolve the yeast in the lukewarm water in a large mixing bowl. Add the olive oil, 2 tablespoons vegetable oil, sugar and salt. Add 1 1/2 cups of the flour. Beat at medium speed for 2 minutes or until the dough leaves the side of the bowl and forms a ball. Add the remaining flour 1/2 cup at a time, mixing well after each addition. The dough will become stiff.

- Knead on a lightly floured surface for 10 minutes or until smooth and elastic. Place in an oiled bowl, turning to grease the surface. Cover with oiled plastic wrap. Let rise for 1 hour or until doubled in bulk. Punch the dough down.

- Oil a 13×18-inch baking sheet and sprinkle with the cornmeal. Place the dough in the center. Press the dough to the edges of the baking sheet using your fingers. Let rise for 30 minutes.

- Preheat the oven to 375 degrees.

- Mix the garlic and 2 tablespoons vegetable oil in a small bowl. Brush lightly over the dough. Sprinkle with the rosemary and kosher salt.

- Bake for 30 minutes or until crisp and golden brown.

Serves 10 to 12

Potato Focaccia

1 medium baking potato, peeled,
   cut into quarters
   (about 9 ounces)
1 1/2 teaspoons fast-rising yeast
3 1/2 cups unbleached flour
1 cup warm water
2 tablespoons olive oil
1 1/4 teaspoons salt
2 tablespoons olive oil
2 tablespoons chopped fresh
   rosemary
1 1/4 teaspoons kosher salt

- Cook the potato in water to cover in a small saucepan for 25 minutes or until tender. Drain the potato, reserving 1/2 cup liquid. Mash the potato. Measure 1 1/3 cups lightly packed potato, reserving any remaining potato for another purpose.

- Combine the yeast, 1/2 cup of the flour and the reserved potato liquid in a large mixing bowl and mix well. Cover tightly and let stand for 20 minutes or until bubbly.

- Add 1 1/3 cups mashed potato, the remaining flour, water, 2 tablespoons olive oil and salt and mix well.

- Knead on a lightly floured surface until smooth and elastic. Place in a greased bowl, turning to coat the surface. Cover and let rise for 1 hour or until the dough is doubled in bulk.

- Place the dough in a generously oiled 10×15-inch baking pan. Press the dough flat using wet hands. Cover with lightly greased plastic wrap. Let rise in a warm place for 45 minutes or until doubled in bulk.

- Preheat the oven to 425 degrees.

- Press dimples in the dough at regular intervals using 2 wet fingers, making sure the dimples are deep enough to hold the olive oil and seasonings. Drizzle the dough with 2 tablespoons olive oil. Sprinkle with the rosemary and kosher salt.

- Bake for 23 to 25 minutes or until the bottom is golden brown and crisp. Remove to a wire rack to cool slightly.

- Cut into desired shapes or wedges. Serve warm.

- Note: Focaccia can be reheated just before serving. You can also shape into two 8-inch rounds before baking.

Makes 3 dozen

Buttermilk Sage Breadsticks

Terrific.

2 cups unbleached flour
1 tablespoon sugar
2 teaspoons rubbed sage
1 teaspoon baking powder
1/2 teaspoon salt
1/2 teaspoon red pepper
1 envelope fast-rising yeast
2 tablespoons shortening
2/3 cup to 1 cup warm buttermilk
2 teaspoons buttermilk

- Combine the flour, sugar, sage, baking powder, salt, red pepper and yeast in a large bowl and whisk to mix well. Cut in the shortening with a pastry blender until crumbly. Add enough of the 2/3 cup warm buttermilk gradually until the dough leaves the side of the bowl and forms a ball, stirring constantly.

- Knead lightly on a lightly floured surface 5 times. Shape into a ball. Roll into a 6×14-inch rectangle. Cut into 14 strips 1 inch wide. Brush with 2 teaspoons buttermilk. Pick up both ends of each strip gently and twist. Place 1 inch apart on a baking sheet coated with nonstick cooking spray. Cover and let rise in a warm place for 20 minutes or until puffy.

- Preheat the oven to 425 degrees.

- Bake for 4 minutes or until golden brown. Remove to a wire rack to cool.

Makes 14 breadsticks

Cheese Buttons

Mini popovers.

1 egg
1/2 cup milk
1/4 cup finely shredded Pepper
    Jack cheese, or 2 tablespoons
    freshly grated Parmesan
    cheese
1/2 cup flour

- Preheat the oven to 400 degrees.

- Spray eighteen 1 3/4-inch muffin cups with nonstick cooking spray. Whisk the egg, milk and cheese in a bowl until well mixed. Add the flour and beat well.

- Fill the prepared muffin cups 1/2 full.

- Bake for 25 minutes.

- Note: To freeze, arrange in a single layer on a baking sheet and freeze until firm. Place in a sealable plastic freezer bag. Store in the freezer for up to 3 months. To serve, heat on a baking sheet in a preheated 400-degree oven for 5 to 6 minutes or until heated through.

Makes 18 mini popovers

Angel Biscuits

Sort of a biscuit-roll—a little sweet. A good bread to serve with Creamed Chicken on page 92.

1 envelope dry yeast
1/4 cup warm water
2 1/2 cups flour
1/2 teaspoon baking soda
1 teaspoon salt
1 teaspoon baking powder
2 tablespoons sugar
1/2 cup shortening
1 cup (about) buttermilk

- Preheat the oven to 400 degrees.

- Dissolve the yeast in the warm water in a small bowl.

- Mix the flour, baking soda, salt, baking powder and sugar in a large bowl. Cut in the shortening with a pastry blender until crumbly. Stir in the yeast mixture and buttermilk.

- Knead on a lightly floured surface 2 or 3 times. Roll into a circle. Cut with a biscuit cutter. Arrange on a baking sheet.

- Bake for 8 to 10 minutes or until golden brown.

- Note: These biscuits freeze well. Place the uncooked biscuits on a baking sheet and freeze. Place in a sealable plastic freezer bag and return to the freezer. When ready to serve, remove the number of biscuits needed and arrange on a greased baking sheet. Cover and let thaw and rise for about 5 hours. Bake as directed above.

Makes about 1 dozen

Buttermilk Biscuits

2 cups flour
1/2 teaspoon salt
1 tablespoon baking powder
1/2 teaspoon baking soda
1/3 cup shortening
1 cup (about) buttermilk

- Preheat the oven to 450 degrees.

- Mix the flour, salt, baking powder and baking soda in a bowl using a whisk. Cut in the shortening with a pastry blender until crumbly. Stir in enough buttermilk gradually to make a soft dough.

- Knead on a lightly floured surface 2 times or until the dough comes together. Pat or roll into a circle. Cut with a biscuit cutter. Arrange on an ungreased baking sheet.

- Bake for 10 to 15 minutes or until brown.

Makes about 1 dozen

Corn Bread

This is Kiki's recipe that I have used for many years. It is the best.

2 tablespoons shortening
1 cup cornmeal
1 cup flour
2 tablespoons sugar
1 1/2 teaspoons salt
1/2 teaspoon baking soda
1 teaspoon baking powder
1 1/4 cups buttermilk
2 eggs, beaten

- Preheat the oven to 450 degrees.

- Heat a cast-iron skillet in the preheated oven. Remove the skillet from the oven. Add the shortening. Return to the oven. Heat until the shortening melts and sizzles.

- Combine the cornmeal, flour, sugar, salt, baking soda, baking powder, buttermilk and eggs in a large bowl and mix well. Add the hot melted shortening and mix well. Pour into the hot skillet.

- Bake for 10 to 20 minutes or until golden brown.

- Serve piping hot with lots of butter.

Serves 8

Cheese-Topped French Bread

6 tablespoons butter
1/2 cup freshly grated Romano
   cheese
1/2 cup freshly grated Parmesan
   cheese
1 tablespoon parsley flakes
1/4 teaspoon garlic powder
6 ounces mozzarella cheese,
   sliced
1 loaf French bread, split into
   halves lengthwise

- Preheat the oven to 375 degrees.

- Melt the butter in a saucepan. Stir in the Romano cheese, Parmesan cheese, parsley flakes and garlic powder.

- Layer the mozzarella cheese over the cut surfaces of the bread. Spread the butter mixture over the top. Arrange on a baking sheet.

- Bake for 10 to 15 minutes or until the cheese is bubbly and the edges of the bread are toasty.

- Cut into slices and serve hot.

Serves 6 to 8

Apple Nut Bread

So moist and flavorful.

4 cups flour
2 teaspoons baking soda
1 teaspoon salt
1 teaspoon nutmeg
2 teaspoons cinnamon
4 eggs
2 cups sugar
1 cup vegetable oil
1/4 cup sour cream
2 cups finely chopped peeled apples
1 cup chopped pecans
1 teaspoon vanilla extract

- Preheat the oven to 350 degrees.

- Mix the flour, baking soda, salt, nutmeg and cinnamon together.

- Beat the eggs in a mixing bowl until frothy. Add the sugar gradually and beat until light and fluffy. Add the flour mixture alternately with the oil and sour cream, beating well after each addition. Stir in the apples, pecans and vanilla.

- Spoon into 2 greased and floured 5×9-inch loaf pans.

- Bake for 1 hour or until a wooden pick inserted in the center comes out clean. Cool in the pans for 5 minutes. Invert onto wire racks to cool completely.

Makes 2 loaves

Apricot Nut Bread

This bread is wonderful when spread with softened cream cheese flavored with a small amount of apricot brandy.

1/2 cup diced dried apricots
2 cups sifted flour
1 tablespoon baking powder
1/4 teaspoon baking soda
3/4 teaspoon salt
1 egg
1 cup sugar
2 tablespoons butter, melted
1/2 cup strained orange juice
1/4 cup water
1 cup sliced almonds

- Soak the apricots in water to cover in a bowl for 30 minutes; drain. Process in a blender until ground.

- Preheat the oven to 350 degrees.

- Sift the flour, baking powder, baking soda and salt together.

- Beat the egg in a mixing bowl until light and fluffy. Add the sugar and mix well. Stir in the butter. Add the flour mixture alternately with the orange juice and water, beating well after each addition. Stir in the almonds and ground apricots.

- Spoon into a greased 5×9-inch loaf pan. Bake for 1 1/2 hours.

- Note: You may bake in 3 or 4 smaller loaf pans, but reduce the baking time.

Makes 1 loaf

Banana Bread

1³/4 cups sifted flour
1 teaspoon baking soda
1/2 teaspoon salt
1/4 cup shortening
1 cup sugar
2 eggs
1 cup mashed bananas (2 large)
1/4 cup sour cream
1/2 cup chopped nuts
1 teaspoon vanilla extract

- Preheat the oven to 350 degrees.

- Mix the flour, baking soda and salt in a bowl using a whisk.

- Cream the shortening and sugar in a mixing bowl until light and fluffy. Beat in the eggs. Add the bananas and sour cream alternately with the flour mixture, beating well after each addition. Stir in the nuts and vanilla.

- Pour into a greased and floured 5×9-inch loaf pan.

- Bake for 1 hour or until the loaf tests done.

Makes 1 loaf

Peach Bread

2 cups sliced fresh peaches
2³/4 cups flour
1¹/2 teaspoons baking powder
1 teaspoon salt
1/2 teaspoon baking soda
1¹/2 teaspoons cinnamon
1/2 cup (1 stick) butter, softened
1 cup sugar
3 eggs
3 tablespoons thawed frozen
    orange juice concentrate
1 teaspoon vanilla extract

- Preheat the oven to 350 degrees.

- Process the peaches in a blender until smooth.

- Mix the flour, baking powder, salt, baking soda and cinnamon together.

- Cream the butter in a mixing bowl. Add the sugar gradually, beating well after each addition. Add the eggs 1 at a time, beating until fluffy. Add the flour mixture and mix well. Fold in the peaches, orange juice concentrate and vanilla. Pour into 2 greased and floured 5×9-inch loaf pans.

- Bake for 1 hour or until a wooden pick inserted in the center comes out clean. Cool in the pans for 5 minutes. Invert onto wire racks to cool completely.

Makes 2 loaves

Pear Bread

2 cups flour
1/2 cup wheat germ
1/2 cup packed brown sugar
1 tablespoon baking powder
1 teaspoon salt
1/4 teaspoon coriander
1 cup lemon yogurt
2 eggs
1/3 cup milk
1/4 cup vegetable oil
1 1/2 cups chopped canned or
    very ripe pears

- Preheat the oven to 350 degrees.

- Mix the flour, wheat germ, brown sugar, baking powder, salt and coriander together.

- Combine the yogurt, eggs, milk and oil in a large bowl and mix well. Add the flour mixture and mix well. Fold in the pears.

- Pour into a greased and floured 5×9-inch loaf pan.

- Bake for 1 hour or until the loaf tests done. Cover loosely with foil if the bread begins to brown too soon.

Makes 1 loaf

Blackberry Sour Cream Coffee Cake

1/2 cup (1 stick) butter, softened
1 cup sugar
3 eggs, lightly beaten
1 teaspoon baking powder
1/4 teaspoon salt
1 teaspoon baking soda
2 cups flour
1 cup sour cream
2 cups fresh or frozen blackberries
1 cup packed brown sugar
1/4 cup (1/2 stick) butter, softened
1/4 cup flour

- Preheat the oven to 350 degrees.

- Cream 1/2 cup butter and sugar in a mixing bowl until light and fluffy. Add the eggs, baking powder, salt and baking soda and beat well. Add 2 cups flour alternately with the sour cream, beating well after each addition. Fold in the blackberries.

- Pour into a greased 9×13-inch baking pan.

- Beat the brown sugar and 1/4 cup butter in a mixing bowl until light and fluffy. Add 1/4 cup flour and mix until crumbly. Sprinkle over the batter.

- Bake for 30 minutes or until the coffee cake tests done. The topping should melt and partially sink into the batter.

Serves 12

Golden Yogurt Coffee Cake

Yummy coffee cake.

Streusel Filling:
1/4 cup sugar
1 tablespoon butter, melted
1 tablespoon flour
1 teaspoon cinnamon
1/4 cup chopped nuts

Coffee Cake:
1 tablespoon butter
1 tablespoon brown sugar
1/4 teaspoon cinnamon
2 apples, cored, sliced
2 cups flour
1 teaspoon baking powder
1 teaspoon baking soda
1/2 teaspoon salt
1/2 cup (1 stick) butter, softened
1/2 cup sugar
2 eggs
1 cup plain yogurt

- Preheat the oven to 350 degrees.

- For the streusel filling, mix 1/4 cup sugar, 1 tablespoon butter, 1 tablespoon flour, 1 teaspoon cinnamon and the nuts in a bowl.

- For the coffee cake, mix 1 tablespoon butter, 1 tablespoon brown sugar and 1/4 teaspoon cinnamon in a 9×9-inch baking pan. Smooth evenly over the bottom. Arrange the apples over the brown sugar mixture.

- Mix 2 cups flour, the baking powder, baking soda and salt together.

- Cream 1/2 cup butter and 1/2 cup sugar in a mixing bowl until light and fluffy. Add the eggs 1 at a time, beating well after each addition. Add the flour mixture alternately with the yogurt, beating well after each addition.

- Spread 1/2 of the batter over the apple slices. Sprinkle with the streusel filling. Spread the remaining batter over the filling.

- Bake for 30 to 35 minutes or until a wooden pick inserted in the center comes out clean.

- Invert onto a serving plate. Serve warm.

Serves 8

Pecan-Topped Coffee Cake

Easy, overnight, light-as-a-feather coffee cake.

2 cups flour
1 teaspoon baking powder
1 teaspoon baking soda
1/2 teaspoon salt
1 teaspoon cinnamon
2/3 cup butter, softened
1 cup sugar
1/2 cup packed brown sugar
2 eggs
1 teaspoon vanilla extract
1 cup buttermilk
1 cup coarsely chopped pecans
1/2 cup packed brown sugar
1/2 teaspoon cinnamon

- Mix the flour, baking powder, baking soda, salt and 1 teaspoon cinnamon together. Cream the butter in a mixing bowl. Add the sugar and 1/2 cup brown sugar gradually, beating well after each addition. Add the eggs 1 at a time, beating well after each addition. Stir in the vanilla.

- Add the flour mixture alternately with the buttermilk, mixing well after each addition and beginning and ending with the flour mixture. Pour into a greased and floured 9×13-inch baking pan.

- Mix the pecans, 1/2 cup brown sugar and 1/2 teaspoon cinnamon in a bowl. Sprinkle over the batter. Cover and chill for 8 to 12 hours. Uncover the batter and bring to room temperature.

- Preheat the oven to 350 degrees. Bake for 35 minutes or until a wooden pick inserted in the center comes out clean.

Serves 15

Plum Coffee Cake

One of my favorites.

3 medium purple plums, chopped
  (1 1/2 cups)
1/4 cup sugar
1 tablespoon cornstarch
1/2 cup (1 stick) butter, softened
3/4 cup sugar
2 eggs
1/3 cup milk
2 cups flour
2 teaspoons baking powder
1/2 teaspoon salt
1/4 to 1/2 teaspoon cinnamon
2 tablespoons sugar
1/4 teaspoon cinnamon

- Preheat the oven to 350 degrees. Mix the plums, 1/4 cup sugar and the cornstarch in a bowl. Cream the butter and 3/4 cup sugar in a mixing bowl until light and fluffy. Add the eggs, milk, flour, baking powder, salt and 1/4 to 1/2 teaspoon cinnamon and beat well.

- Pour 1/2 of the batter into a greased and floured 8-inch springform pan. Top with the plum mixture. Spoon the remaining batter over the plum mixture, being sure to cover. Sprinkle with a mixture of 2 tablespoons sugar and 1/4 teaspoon cinnamon.

- Bake for 1 hour or until the coffee cake tests done, covering loosely with foil after 40 minutes to prevent overbrowning.

- Remove from the oven. Let stand until partially cooled. Remove the side of the pan. Cut into wedges and serve warm or at room temperature.

Serves 8 to 10

Calico Crumb Cake

A quick, tasty cake for breakfast or light supper dessert. Believe me, everyone will love this cake. Take this warm cake to a new mother or elderly friend (who can eat sweets), or just to a neighborhood coffee.

1/2 cup flour
1/3 cup brown sugar
1/4 cup (1/2 stick) butter
1/2 cup chopped nuts
1 cup (6 ounces) chocolate chips
1/2 cup shortening
2 cups flour
1 teaspoon baking soda
1/2 teaspoon salt
1 cup sugar
2 eggs
1 cup buttermilk
1 teaspoon vanilla extract

- Preheat the oven to 350 degrees.

- Mix 1/2 cup flour and the brown sugar in a bowl. Cut in the butter until crumbly. Stir in the nuts.

- Melt the chocolate chips, covered, in a double boiler over very hot water.

- Beat the shortening, 2 cups flour, the baking soda, salt, sugar, eggs, buttermilk and vanilla in a mixing bowl until smooth.

- Pour into a greased 9×13-inch baking pan. Drizzle the chocolate over the batter. Cut through with a knife to swirl. Sprinkle with the crumb mixture.

- Bake for 35 to 40 minutes. Serve warm.

Serves 15

Banana Muffins

Just a little different, in a good sort of way.

1 1/2 cups flour
1 cup sugar
1/2 teaspoon salt
1/2 teaspoon cinnamon
1/2 teaspoon baking soda
1/4 teaspoon baking powder
4 egg whites
1/2 cup vegetable oil
1 1/2 teaspoons vanilla extract
1 cup mashed bananas
1/4 cup yogurt
1/2 cup golden raisins

- Preheat the oven to 350 degrees.

- Sift the flour, sugar, salt, cinnamon, baking soda and baking powder into a bowl or mix with a whisk.

- Stir in the egg whites, oil and vanilla. Add the bananas, yogurt and raisins and stir until combined. Pour into paper-lined muffin cups.

- Bake for 20 to 25 minutes or until the muffins test done.

Makes 1 dozen

Chocolate Cherry Muffins

1/2 cup boiling water
3/4 cup dried cherries
3 ounces unsweetened chocolate
3 ounces dark chocolate
1/4 cup (1/2 stick) unsalted butter
1/2 cup flour
1/2 teaspoon baking powder
1/4 teaspoon salt
2 eggs
1/2 cup sugar
1 teaspoon vanilla extract
1 teaspoon instant coffee powder
1/2 cup coarsely chopped dark
   chocolate

- Preheat the oven to 350 degrees.

- Pour the boiling water over the dried cherries in a small bowl.
  Let stand for 5 minutes; drain.

- Melt the unsweetened chocolate, 3 ounces dark chocolate
  and butter in a double boiler over simmering water, stirring
  frequently. Remove from the heat to cool slightly.

- Mix the flour, baking powder and salt together.

- Beat the eggs, sugar, vanilla and coffee powder in a mixing bowl
  until light and nearly doubled in volume. Beat in the chocolate
  mixture. Add the flour mixture and beat until blended. Stir in
  1/2 cup chopped dark chocolate and cherries.

- Spoon into buttered or paper-lined muffin cups, filling each cup
  about 3/4 full and smoothing the top.

- Bake for 13 to 15 minutes or until dry on top. Do not overbake.
  The centers should remain moist. Cool in the pans for 10 minutes.
  Remove to wire racks to cool completely.

Makes 1 dozen

Mandarin Almond Spice Muffins

Great.

3/4 cup all-purpose flour
3/4 cup whole wheat flour
1/2 cup sugar
1/2 cup chopped slivered almonds
2 teaspoons baking powder
1/2 teaspoon salt
1/4 teaspoon nutmeg
1/4 teaspoon allspice
1/4 cup (1/2 stick) butter, melted
1/2 cup milk
1 egg, lightly beaten
1/2 teaspoon almond extract
1 (11-ounce) can mandarin
   oranges, drained, chopped
3 tablespoons butter, melted
1/3 cup sugar
1 1/2 teaspoons cinnamon

- Preheat the oven to 400 degrees.

- Mix the all-purpose flour, whole wheat flour, 1/2 cup sugar, almonds, baking powder, salt, nutmeg and allspice in a large bowl.

- Combine 1/4 cup butter, milk, egg and almond extract in a small bowl and mix well. Add to the flour mixture and stir until moistened. Stir in the mandarin oranges gently. Spoon into 12 greased muffin cups.

- Bake for 15 to 20 minutes or until light golden brown.

- Place 3 tablespoons butter in a small shallow bowl. Mix 1/3 cup sugar and cinnamon in a shallow bowl.

- Dip the tops of the warm muffins in the butter; dip in the sugar mixture. Serve warm.

Makes 1 dozen

Tiny Orange Muffins

A sprig of mock orange is a nice touch.

1/2 cup (1 stick) butter, softened
1 cup sugar
2 eggs
1 teaspoon baking soda
1 cup buttermilk
2 cups unbleached flour
Grated zest of 2 oranges
1/2 cup golden raisins
Juice of 2 oranges
1 cup packed brown sugar

- Preheat the oven to 400 degrees.

- Cream the butter and sugar in a mixing bowl until light and fluffy. Add the eggs and beat well.

- Dissolve the baking soda in the buttermilk in a small bowl. Add to the creamed mixture alternately with the flour, beating well after each addition. Stir in the orange zest and raisins. Fill paper-lined miniature muffin cups 3/4 full.

- Bake for 15 minutes. Remove immediately to a serving plate and keep warm.

- Mix the orange juice and brown sugar in a bowl. Pour 1 teaspoon of the mixture over each muffin. Top with additional grated orange zest if desired.

Makes 4 to 5 dozen

*Failure is the opportunity to begin again
more intelligently.*
—Henry Ford

White Chocolate Apricot Muffins

1³/4 cups flour
¹/2 cup sugar
1 tablespoon minced candied ginger
1¹/2 teaspoons baking powder
¹/2 teaspoon salt
2 ounces white chocolate, finely
    chopped
³/4 cup milk
3 tablespoons butter, melted
1 egg, lightly beaten
¹/2 cup apricot preserves
1 tablespoon sugar

- Preheat the oven to 400 degrees.

- Combine the flour, ¹/2 cup sugar, ginger, baking powder, salt and white chocolate in a medium bowl and stir with a whisk to mix well. Make a well in the center.

- Beat the milk, butter and egg in a bowl using a whisk. Add to the well in the flour mixture and stir until moistened.

- Spoon about 1 tablespoon batter into each of 12 muffin cups sprayed with nonstick cooking spray. Spoon 2 teaspoons preserves into the center of each. Top with the remaining batter. Sprinkle evenly with 1 tablespoon sugar.

- Bake for 22 minutes or until the muffins spring back when lightly touched in the center. Remove from the pan to wire racks to cool completely.

Makes 1 dozen

Imagination is intelligence having fun.

Blackberry Butter

1/2 cup (1 stick) butter, softened
2 tablespoons seedless blackberry
    jam
1/3 cup finely chopped pecans

- Beat the butter, blackberry jam and pecans in a small bowl until blended.

- Chill, covered, for 8 hours.

- Note: Melt the butter and pour into molds for a nice effect at mealtime.

Makes about 3/4 cup

Strawberry Honey Butter

1 pint strawberries
3 tablespoons honey
1 teaspoon sugar
1 teaspoon fresh lime juice
3/4 cup (1 1/2 sticks) butter,
    softened

- Purée the strawberries in a blender. Strain the strawberries, discarding the seeds.

- Combine the strained strawberries, honey, sugar and lime juice in a medium saucepan. Boil for 3 minutes or until thickened, stirring constantly. Remove from the heat. Cool to room temperature.

- Combine the strawberry mixture and butter in a medium bowl and mix well. Let stand, covered, for 1 hour.

- Serve with your favorite scone, biscuit or roll.

Makes about 1 1/2 cups

Breakfast Entrées

You prepare a meal for me in
front of my enemies.
You pour oil on my head,
you fill my cup to overflowing.
Surely your goodness and
love will be with me all
my life, and I will live in the
house of the Lord forever.

Psalm 23:5-6
New Century Version

Best Buttermilk Pancakes

2 cups flour
3 tablespoons sugar
2 teaspoons baking powder
1 teaspoon baking soda
1/2 teaspoon salt
2 eggs, lightly beaten
3 cups buttermilk
1/4 cup (1/2 stick) butter, melted
Butter for brushing
1 cup fresh fruit, such as
    blueberries or strawberries,
    or nuts

- Preheat the griddle to 375 degrees.

- Combine the flour, sugar, baking powder, baking soda and salt in a bowl and whisk to mix well. Add the eggs, buttermilk and 1/4 cup melted butter and whisk to mix well. Do not overbeat. The batter should have small lumps.

- Brush about 1/2 teaspoon butter onto the griddle using a pastry brush. Wipe off the excess. Pour about 1/3 cup of the batter at a time 2 inches apart on the prepared griddle. Sprinkle with the fruit.

- Cook until brown on both sides.

- Serve with maple syrup.

- Note: You may prepare ahead of time and reheat in a preheated 350-degree oven for 3 minutes.

Makes nine 6-inch pancakes

Oatmeal Pancakes

*These pancakes are delicious when sautéed thin slices of apple are
added to the pancakes on the griddle before turning over.*

2 cups rolled oats
2 cups buttermilk
1/2 cup flour
3 tablespoons sugar
1 teaspoon baking powder
1 teaspoon baking soda
2 eggs, beaten
1/4 cup (1/2 stick) butter, melted

- Combine the oats and buttermilk in a bowl and mix well. Let stand, covered, in the refrigerator for 8 to 10 hours.

- Preheat the griddle.

- Sift the flour, sugar, baking powder and baking soda into the oat mixture. Add the eggs and butter and mix well.

- Pour the desired amount of the batter onto the hot griddle for each pancake. Cook until bubbles appear on the surface and the underside is golden brown. Turn the pancake. Cook until golden brown. Repeat with the remaining batter.

- Serve with cinnamon-sugar and/or pure maple syrup.

Makes 16 pancakes

Pancakes with Fresh Apricot Sauce

We also enjoy this recipe with spiced pear butter.

Fresh Apricot Sauce:
12 fresh apricots
4 oranges, cut into sections
1/2 cup or more apricot preserves
2 tablespoons Grand Marnier
2 tablespoons cornstarch
  (optional)

Pancakes:
1 cup unbleached flour
1 teaspoon baking powder
1/2 teaspoon baking soda
1/2 teaspoon salt
2 tablespoons sugar
1 egg
1 cup milk
3 tablespoons apricot preserves
2 tablespoons unsalted butter,
  melted

- For the sauce, rinse the apricots and pat dry. Cut the apricots into halves and discard the pits. Cut the apricots into slices.

- Combine the apricots, oranges and apricot preserves in a saucepan and mix well. Bring to a boil, stirring frequently. Stir in the Grand Marnier. Thicken with cornstarch if desired.

- Preheat the griddle.

- For the pancakes, mix the flour, baking powder, baking soda, salt and sugar in a large bowl. Whisk the egg, milk, apricot preserves and butter in a bowl until smooth. Fold into the flour mixture.

- Pour about 1/3 cup batter onto the hot griddle. Cook until bubbles appear on the surface and the underside is golden brown. Turn the pancake. Cook for 1 minute or until golden brown. Repeat with the remaining batter.

- Serve with the sauce.

Serves 3 or 4

German Pancakes

We bake our pancakes in individual cast-iron skillets, so that each guest is served his or her very own German pancake and can add toppings or fillings of choice.

3 eggs
3/4 cup flour
3/4 cup milk
1/2 teaspoon salt
1/2 teaspoon vanilla extract
1 1/2 tablespoons butter

- Preheat the oven to 450 degrees.

- Beat the eggs, flour, milk, salt and vanilla in a mixing bowl until smooth.

- Melt the butter in a 12-inch cast-iron skillet in the oven. Add the batter.

- Bake for 15 minutes. Reduce the oven temperature to 350 degrees. Bake for 10 minutes longer. The pancake will puff dramatically but will soon settle down. Serve your guests immediately so they can enjoy the actual beauty of the pancake. The side will end up higher than the middle, making a crater for fillings or toppings.

Serves 2

Many people enjoy squeezing the juice of 1 lemon over the pancake and sprinkling with confectioners' sugar to taste. Or, try one of the fruit fillings below that we enjoy at Peacock Hill.

Apple Filling:
- Peel 4 or 5 Granny Smith apples and cut into slices. Sauté the apples in 1/4 cup (1/2 stick) butter. Sprinkle with a mixture of 1/4 cup packed brown sugar, a dash of cinnamon and a dash of nutmeg. Cook until the apples are just heated through and tender, but not mushy. Spoon over the pancake and sprinkle with confectioners' sugar.

Peach Filling:
- Peel 4 to 6 peaches and cut into slices, discarding the pits. Sauté the peaches in a skillet for 4 to 6 minutes, depending upon their ripeness. Remove from the heat and add a tiny drop of almond extract. We add brown sugar as a sweetener, but not too much.

Lemon juice is probably the best topping for this pancake. Toasted pecan pieces are also quite good. My favorite topping is a bowl of dried apricots that have been soaked overnight in light tea water and then heated the next morning until soft. Serve with plain or vanilla yogurt. Yum!

Honey Puff Pancake

Honey Butter:
1/2 cup honey
1/2 cup confectioners' sugar
1/2 cup (1 stick) butter, softened
Cinnamon to taste

Pancakes:
3 tablespoons butter
6 eggs, at room temperature
1 cup milk
3 tablespoons honey
3 ounces cream cheese, softened
1 cup flour
1/2 teaspoon salt
1/2 teaspoon baking powder

- For the honey butter, beat 1/2 cup honey, the confectioners' sugar, 1/2 cup butter and the cinnamon in a bowl until smooth.

- Preheat the oven to 400 degrees.

- For the pancakes, grease a 10-inch skillet with 1 tablespoon of the butter. Place the remaining 2 tablespoons butter in the skillet. Place in the oven. Watch carefully and remove when the butter is melted and sizzles.

- Process the eggs, milk, 3 tablespoons honey, cream cheese, flour, salt and baking powder in a blender at high speed for 1 minute or until smooth. Pour into the hot butter in the skillet.

- Bake for 20 to 25 minutes or until puffed and golden brown. Spread a small amount of the honey butter over the pancake.

- Serve with a sprinkle of confectioners' sugar and pass the remaining honey butter.

Serves 6

Then you add two forkfuls of cooking oil.
—The Low-Fat Chef

53

Banana Waffles

These waffles freeze nicely. Just reheat in a toaster and serve.

Pecan Maple Syrup:
1/2 cup pure maple syrup
1/4 cup chopped toasted pecans
2 teaspoons orange juice

Waffles:
1/3 cup flour
1/3 cup cornmeal
1 tablespoon sugar
2 teaspoons baking powder
1/4 teaspoon salt
1 medium ripe banana
1/3 cup water
2 eggs
2 tablespoons butter, melted,
    cooled
Vegetable oil for brushing

- For the syrup, bring the maple syrup and pecans to a boil in a small saucepan. Stir in the orange juice. Remove from the heat. Cover and keep warm.

- For the waffles, whisk the flour, cornmeal, sugar, baking powder and salt together in a bowl.

- Peel the banana and cut into quarters. Purée the banana and water in a blender.

- Whisk the banana purée, eggs and butter together in a bowl. Add the flour mixture and stir until well combined.

- Preheat the waffle iron.

- Brush the hot waffle iron lightly with oil. Pour 1/2 of the batter into the prepared waffle iron. Cook using the manufacturer's instructions. Repeat with the remaining batter.

- Serve immediately with the syrup.

Serves 2

Wonderful Yogurt Waffles

1/2 cup (1 stick) butter, melted
3/4 cup milk
3/4 cup plain or vanilla yogurt
3 eggs
1 teaspoon vanilla extract
2 teaspoons baking powder
3/4 teaspoon baking soda
1/2 teaspoon salt
1 1/2 cups flour

- Preheat a Belgian waffle iron.

- Combine the butter, milk, yogurt, eggs, vanilla, baking powder, baking soda, salt and flour in the order listed in a bowl and whisk until blended. The batter will be lumpy.

- Pour 3/4 cup of the batter into the preheated waffle iron.

- Cook until the steam disappears and the waffle is brown.

- Repeat with the remaining batter.

Serves 6 to 8

Applesauce

Makes a great side dish for breakfast sausage and French toast or even pork or chicken.

10 tart apples, peeled, cored,
    chopped
3/4 cup packed brown sugar
1/2 cup apple cider
1 1/2 teaspoons cinnamon
1/8 teaspoon nutmeg
1/8 teaspoon salt

- Combine the apples, brown sugar, apple cider, cinnamon, nutmeg and salt in a saucepan and mix well.

- Cook over medium heat for 40 to 50 minutes or until the desired consistency, stirring frequently.

Makes 1 1/2 to 2 cups

Peachy Cherry Sauce

1/4 cup sugar
2 tablespoons cornstarch
Dash of salt
1/2 cup water
1 (10-ounce) package frozen
    sliced peaches
1 cup frozen tart cherries
1 tablespoon butter
2 tablespoons Cointreau or
    apricot brandy

- Combine the sugar, cornstarch and salt in a saucepan and mix well. Stir in the water.

- Cook over low heat until the sauce thickens and clears, stirring constantly. Stir in the peaches and cherries.

- Cook until the peaches are soft. Stir in the butter and Cointreau.

- Serve hot over waffles or pancakes with whipped cream or sour cream on top.

Makes about 2 cups

Oven-Fried Bacon

12 slices bacon

- Preheat the oven to 400 degrees.

- Arrange the bacon in a large shallow baking pan. Place on the medium oven rack.

- Bake for 5 to 6 minutes or until the fat begins to render. Rotate the pan from front to back. Bake for 5 to 6 minutes longer or until the bacon is brown and crisp. Remove the bacon with tongs to paper towels to drain.

- Note: Bake for 8 to 10 minutes longer or until brown and crisp if the bacon is thickly sliced.

Serves 4 to 6

Bacon and Potato Omelet

2 Yukon Gold potatoes
Salt to taste
4 eggs
1 tablespoon sour cream
Pepper to taste
6 slices bacon, chopped
1 small onion, chopped
2 tablespoons minced fresh parsley
2 tablespoons minced fresh chives

- Cook the potatoes in salted boiling water to cover in a saucepan for 15 minutes or until tender; drain. Peel and cut into slices 1/4-inch thick.

- Preheat the broiler.

- Beat the eggs in a medium bowl until blended. Add the sour cream, salt and pepper to taste and mix well.

- Sauté the bacon in a 10-inch skillet until crisp and brown. Remove to paper towels to drain. Drain the pan drippings, reserving 2 tablespoons of the drippings in the skillet.

- Add the onion and potatoes to the reserved drippings in the skillet. Sauté until glazed. Pour the egg mixture over the vegetable mixture. Sprinkle with the bacon.

- Reduce the heat to low. Cook until the eggs are set, carefully moving the potatoes and eggs to keep them from sticking. This is hard to do. Broil until heated through. Watch carefully.

- Sprinkle with the parsley and chives. Slide onto a serving platter. Cut into wedges to serve.

Serves 4

Southern Country Breakfast

Delightful brunch entrée to serve in cool weather.

2 pounds bulk pork sausage
1 cup uncooked grits
1/4 cup (1/2 stick) butter
2 cups shredded sharp Cheddar
   cheese
5 eggs
1 1/2 cups milk
Salt and pepper to taste

- Preheat the oven to 350 degrees.

- Brown the sausage in a skillet, stirring until brown and crumbly; drain. Spread in the bottom of a 9×13-inch baking dish.

- Cook the grits using the package directions until thickened. Add the butter and cheese and mix well. Cool slightly.

- Beat the eggs, milk, salt and pepper in a bowl. Add to the grits mixture and mix well. Pour over the sausage layer.

- Bake for 1 hour or until set. Garnish with chopped fresh thyme.

Serves 8

Peahen's Nest

Simple, but oh, so good.

4 to 6 (1-inch) slices French bread
8 eggs
1 1/3 cups milk
1 cup shredded sharp Cheddar
   cheese
1/4 cup (1/2 stick) butter, cut into
   small pieces
2 tablespoons chopped fresh chives

- Arrange the bread in a single layer in a well-greased baking dish.

- Whisk the eggs and milk together in a bowl. Pour over the bread slices. Sprinkle with the cheese. Arrange the small pieces of butter over the top.

- Cover tightly with plastic wrap. Chill for 8 to 12 hours.

- Preheat the oven to 375 degrees.

- Bake, uncovered, for 20 to 25 minutes or until set. Sprinkle with the chives.

- Serve with crisp bacon.

Serves 4 to 6

Soups and Salads

...our Father in heaven,

may your name

always be kept holy.

May your kingdom come

and what you want

be done, here on earth

as it is in heaven.

Give us the food

we need for each day.

Matthew 6:9-11
New Century Version

Black-Eyed Pea Soup

Spicy, real good and filling.

2 cups or 1 pound dried
  black-eyed peas
1 ham hock
1 large onion, chopped
1 bunch green onions, chopped,
  or 3 leek bulbs, thinly sliced
1 cup chopped green bell pepper
2 garlic cloves, crushed
1 tablespoon Worcestershire
  sauce
1 cup chopped fresh parsley
1/4 teaspoon oregano
1/4 teaspoon thyme
2 bay leaves
1 teaspoon cumin
1 teaspoon salt
1 teaspoon pepper
2 cups undrained tomatoes with
  green chiles

- Sort and rinse the peas. Soak in water to cover in a large saucepan for 8 to 12 hours; drain.

- Add the ham hock, onion, green onions, bell pepper, garlic, Worcestershire sauce, parsley, oregano, thyme, bay leaves, cumin, salt and pepper and mix well. Stir in the undrained tomatoes with green chiles. Add enough water to cover.

- Cook for 8 to 12 hours. Discard the bay leaves before serving.

- Serve over rice with plenty of coleslaw and a cast-iron skillet filled with hot corn bread. Pass the butter and enjoy. (Happy New Year!)

Serves 6 to 8

Prayer Chapel located on one of the trails at Peacock Hill.

Vegetarian Minestrone

This soup is good.

3 medium leeks, chopped
3 garlic cloves, crushed
3 tablespoons olive oil
6 cups vegetable stock or chicken
    broth
1 (15-ounce) can kidney beans,
    drained
1 (16-ounce) can garbanzo
    beans, drained
1 (28-ounce) can tomatoes,
    chopped
2 cups finely chopped cabbage
2 cups chopped potatoes
2 cups cut green beans
1 1/2 cups sliced squash
1 cup chopped carrots
1/2 cup chopped celery
1/4 cup chopped fresh parsley
1/2 teaspoon basil
1/2 teaspoon oregano
1/2 teaspoon rosemary
Salt and pepper to taste
1/4 cup tomato paste
1/2 cup uncooked macaroni

- Sauté the leeks and garlic in the olive oil in a large saucepan for 2 to 5 minutes or until the leeks are tender. Add the vegetable stock, kidney beans, garbanzo beans, tomatoes, cabbage, potatoes, green beans, squash, carrots, celery, parsley, basil, oregano, rosemary, salt and pepper and mix well.

- Bring to a boil and reduce the heat. Simmer for 30 minutes. Stir in the tomato paste and uncooked macaroni.

- Cook for 15 minutes. Ladle into soup bowls. Garnish with freshly grated Parmesan cheese.

- Note: You may add cooked beef to the soup.

Serves 6

Baked Potato Soup

This soup is best made a day ahead, but is delicious anytime.

3 pounds baking potatoes
2 cups chopped celery
2 cups chopped onion
1/4 teaspoon minced garlic
1 tablespoon butter
1/2 cup plus 1 tablespoon flour
2 quarts chicken broth (8 cups)
2 teaspoons basil
1/4 teaspoon pepper
3 cups heavy cream
1/2 cup sour cream
1/4 cup parsley flakes

- Preheat the oven to 400 degrees.

- Scrub the potatoes and pierce with a fork. Place on the oven rack. Bake for 50 minutes or until tender. Sauté the celery, onion and garlic in the butter in a stockpot until tender. Stir in the flour. Add the chicken broth. Simmer for 5 minutes.

- Cut the baked potatoes into halves. Scoop out the pulp and add to the stockpot. Season with the basil and pepper. Mix the cream, sour cream and parsley flakes in a bowl. Add to the soup and stir to mix well.

- Ladle into soup bowls. Garnish with shredded Cheddar cheese and sliced green onions.

Serves 12

Yukon Gold Potato Soup

Yum.

1 garlic bulb
1 teaspoon olive oil
1 1/2 pounds Yukon gold potatoes, scrubbed, chopped
1 large onion, chopped
2 large shallots, chopped
2 carrots, cut into large pieces
5 cups chicken broth
1 teaspoon salt
Sprigs of fresh thyme
Sprigs of fresh rosemary
1 cup light cream
1 cup skim milk
Salt and pepper to taste

- Preheat the oven to 375 degrees.

- Peel the heavier pieces of the skin from the garlic bulb, leaving the cloves and a small amount of the skin attached. Sprinkle with the olive oil. Wrap in foil. Bake for 20 to 30 minutes or until the cloves are soft. Remove from the oven to cool. Remove each clove from the bulb. Squeeze the pulp gently into a bowl.

- Combine the potatoes, onion, shallots, carrots, chicken broth, salt, thyme and rosemary in a large Dutch oven. Bring to a boil. Cover and reduce the heat. Simmer for 20 to 30 minutes or until the carrot and potatoes are tender. Remove and discard the herb sprigs. Mash the potatoes using a potato masher. Add the garlic pulp and mash well.

- Cook for 10 minutes or until the soup is thickened. Stir in the cream and milk. Cook over medium heat until heated through. Season with salt and pepper. Ladle into soup bowls.

Serves 8

Potato Vegetable Soup

A tasty way to clean out the refrigerator.

1 medium onion, chopped
1/2 cup (1 stick) butter
8 potatoes, peeled, chopped
3 tablespoons chicken bouillon
  granules
1/2 cup flour
4 cups half-and-half or milk
1 (10-ounce) package frozen
  green peas
3 tablespoons chopped fresh
  parsley, or 1 tablespoon dried
  parsley
Salt and pepper to taste

- Sauté the onion in the butter in a large saucepan. Add the potatoes and enough water to cover. Add the bouillon granules.

- Cook over medium heat until the potatoes are tender. Reduce the heat.

- Combine the flour and 2 cups of the half-and-half in a jar with a lid. Cover and shake to mix well. Add to the potatoes.

- Cook for 3 to 4 minutes or until thickened, stirring constantly. Add the remaining half-and-half gradually, stirring constantly to prevent scorching. Add the peas, parsley, salt and pepper. Cook until heated through.

- Ladle into soup bowls. Garnish with crumbled crisp bacon.

- Note: You may add any or all of the following vegetables: sautéed mushrooms, green beans, shredded carrots or shredded zucchini.

Serves 6 to 8

*Ham and eggs: A day's work for a chicken,
a lifetime commitment for a pig.*

Tomato Bisque

Easy and tasty.

1 medium onion, chopped
1/4 cup (1/2 stick) butter
1 (10-ounce) can tomato soup
1 (14-ounce) can tomatoes,
    chopped
1 1/3 cups milk
Dash of basil
Dash of thyme
Dash of white pepper
Dash of cayenne pepper

- Sauté the onion in the butter in a large saucepan until tender. Add the tomato soup, undrained tomatoes, milk, basil, thyme, white pepper and cayenne pepper.

- Cook until heated through. Ladle into soup bowls.

Serves 8 small portions

Garden Vegetable Soup

A wonderful way to get all of your vitamins at once.

1 medium onion, chopped
2 tablespoons vegetable oil
6 cups chicken broth
1 bay leaf
3 fresh basil leaves
2 sprigs of fresh parsley
2 (2-inch) strips lemon zest
1 pound tomatoes, chopped
2 cups (1-inch) cubed unpeeled
    red potatoes
1 cup thinly sliced carrots
1 cup diagonally cut green beans
1/2 cup chopped celery
1/2 teaspoon salt
Pepper to taste
Corn kernels from 1 ear of corn,
    or 1 cup frozen whole kernel
    corn
1 cup julienned zucchini

- Sauté the onion in the oil in a stockpot for 3 to 4 minutes or until translucent. Add the chicken broth, bay leaf, basil, parsley, lemon zest, tomatoes, potatoes, carrots, green beans, celery, salt and pepper.

- Bring to a boil over medium heat. Reduce the heat to low and cover. Simmer for 20 minutes, stirring occasionally. Add the corn and zucchini.

- Simmer, covered, for 15 minutes, stirring occasionally. Discard the bay leaf, parsley and lemon zest.

- Ladle into soup bowls.

Serves 4

Spring Chowder

Believe me, you will like it.

1 tablespoon butter
4 cups thinly sliced sweet onions
1 cup (or more) chopped carrots
1 cup (or more) sliced celery
1 cup chopped cooked ham
3 cups chopped red potatoes
1 (10-ounce) can chicken broth
1/4 cup flour
2 cups milk
1/4 cup chopped fresh sage
1/2 teaspoon salt
1/4 to 1/2 teaspoon pepper
1/8 teaspoon nutmeg
1/2 cup dry white wine

- Melt the butter in a large saucepan over medium-high heat. Add the onions, carrots, celery and ham.

- Sauté for 10 minutes. Add the potatoes and chicken broth.

- Bring to a boil. Cover and reduce the heat. Simmer for 10 minutes or until tender.

- Place the flour in a bowl. Add the milk gradually, stirring with a whisk to blend. Add the milk mixture, sage, salt, pepper and nutmeg to the potato mixture.

- Cook over medium-low heat for 2 minutes. Add the wine. Cook for 10 minutes or until thickened, stirring constantly.

- Ladle into 1-cup soup bowls. Garnish with fresh sage leaves.

Serves 8

Chicken Soup with Orzo and Vegetables

A real favorite. Make your own chicken broth if you have time.

1 medium leek
2 tablespoons vegetable oil
1 large carrot, cut into slices
    1/4 inch thick
1 rib celery, cut into slices
    1/4 inch thick
4 ounces asparagus, cut into
    1-inch lengths
1/4 cup fresh or frozen green peas
1/2 teaspoon thyme
6 to 8 cups chicken broth
1/2 cup uncooked orzo
1/4 cup minced fresh parsley, or
    2 tablespoons fresh tarragon
Pepper to taste

- Rinse the leek well. Cut lengthwise into quarters; cut into thin slices crosswise.

- Heat the oil in a stockpot over medium-high heat. Add the leek, carrot and celery. Sauté for 5 minutes or until softened. Add the asparagus, peas, thyme and chicken broth. Simmer for 10 to 12 minutes or until the vegetables are tender.

- Add the orzo. Cook until tender. Stir in the parsley and pepper. Adjust the seasonings to taste.

Serves 6

Green Fruit Salad

Simply fruit and limeade.

1/2 honeydew melon, peeled,
    seeded, cut into chunks
1 1/3 cups whole green grapes
2 kiwifruit, peeled, cut into thick
    slices
2 tablespoons frozen limeade
    concentrate
2 tablespoons minced fresh mint
1/3 cup blackberries, raspberries,
    or a mixture of both

- Combine the honeydew melon, grapes, kiwifruit, limeade concentrate and mint in a large bowl and toss to mix.

- Add the blackberries and toss gently to mix.

- Chill, covered, until ready to serve. Serve slightly chilled.

Serves 4

Mixed Fruit Salad

1 (20-ounce) can pineapple
    chunks
1/2 cup sugar
3 tablespoons flour
1 egg, lightly beaten
2 (11-ounce) cans mandarin
    oranges, drained
1 (20-ounce) can pears, drained,
    chopped
3 kiwifruit, peeled, sliced
2 large unpeeled apples, chopped
1 cup pecan halves

- Drain the pineapple, reserving the juice. Bring the reserved pineapple juice, sugar and flour to a boil in a saucepan, stirring constantly. Add a small amount of the hot mixture to the egg in a bowl. Stir the egg gently into the hot mixture.

- Cook until thickened, stirring constantly. Remove from the heat to cool.

- Chill, covered, in the refrigerator.

- Combine the pineapple, mandarin oranges, pears, kiwifruit, apples and pecans in a large bowl. Add the chilled dressing and toss to coat.

- Chill, covered, for 1 hour.

- Note: You may use chopped fresh pears instead of canned pears.

Serves 12 to 16

Yogurt Fruit Salad

1/2 cup pineapple juice
1 tablespoon flour
4 ounces cream cheese, softened
1/2 cup yogurt
1/2 tablespoon lime juice
3 tablespoons sugar
1/4 teaspoon vanilla extract
6 apples, chopped
1 tablespoon lemon juice
28 red grapes, cut into halves
1 ounce pecans, chopped

- Cook the pineapple juice and flour in a saucepan until thickened, stirring constantly. Remove from the heat to cool completely.

- Combine the cream cheese, yogurt, lime juice, sugar and vanilla in a mixing bowl and beat until smooth.

- Toss the apples with the lemon juice in a bowl.

- Combine the pineapple juice mixture and 1/2 cup of the cream cheese mixture in a bowl and mix well. Add the apple mixture, grapes and pecans and toss to mix well.

- To serve, spoon the salad onto serving plates. Dollop each serving with the remaining cream cheese mixture.

Serves 4

Fresh Fruit Salad

Serve as a salad or as a light dessert with whipped cream and pound cake.

1/2 cup chopped apples
1 cup fresh pineapple chunks
1/2 cup fresh orange sections
1 cup sliced fresh peaches
1 cup sliced fresh strawberries
2 to 3 tablespoons sugar, or
   to taste
2 bananas, sliced
1/4 cup pecan pieces

- Combine the apples, pineapple chunks, orange sections, peaches, strawberries and sugar in a large bowl and toss to mix.

- Chilled, covered, until ready to serve. Add the bananas and pecans just before serving and toss gently.

- Serve with whipped cream.

Serves 6

Molded Fresh Peaches

1 envelope unflavored gelatin
1/4 cup cold water
2 (3-ounce) packages peach
    gelatin
1 1/4 cups boiling water
1 cup orange juice
3 tablespoons fresh lemon juice
1 tablespoon grated lemon zest
1 1/2 cups puréed fresh peaches
3 to 4 tablespoons sugar
    (optional)
3 ounces cream cheese, softened
1 tablespoon mayonnaise
1 peach, puréed

- Soften the unflavored gelatin in the cold water in a bowl. Add the peach gelatin. Add the boiling water and stir until the gelatins are dissolved.

- Stir in the orange juice, lemon juice, lemon zest, 1 1/2 cups peach purée and sugar.

- Spoon into a 1 1/2-quart mold. Chill until set.

- Beat the cream cheese and mayonnaise in a mixing bowl until smooth. Add the puréed peach and mix well.

- To serve, unmold the salad onto a serving plate. Serve with the cream cheese mixture.

Serves 6

Mixed Greens with Oranges and Pecans

This is a favorite at Peacock Hill. It is nice to serve with chicken or pork.

4 heads Bibb lettuce
2 oranges, peeled, sectioned
3/4 cup pecan halves, toasted
1/3 cup red wine vinegar
1/4 cup (about) sugar
1 cup vegetable oil
1 teaspoon salt
1/2 small onion, chopped
1 teaspoon dry mustard
2 tablespoons water

- Rinse the lettuce and pat dry. Tear the lettuce into bite-size pieces into a large salad bowl. Add the oranges and pecans.

- Process the red wine vinegar, sugar, oil, salt, onion, dry mustard and water in a blender until blended.

- Add to the lettuce mixture just before serving and toss to mix. Garnish with additional orange sections and pecans.

- Note: You may also use a mixture of romaine and spinach instead of the Bibb lettuce. If fresh oranges are unavailable, use drained canned mandarin oranges.

Serves 8

Orange Spinach Salad

1 bunch fresh spinach
1 head Boston Bibb lettuce or
   romaine
2 fresh oranges, peeled, chopped
1/2 cup slivered almonds, toasted
1/3 cup canola oil
1/3 cup fresh orange juice
3 tablespoons raspberry vinegar
1 garlic clove, crushed
1 tablespoon sugar
Salt and pepper to taste

- Rinse the spinach and lettuce and pat dry. Tear into bite-size pieces into a salad bowl. Add the oranges and almonds and toss to mix.

- Combine the canola oil, orange juice, raspberry vinegar, garlic, sugar, salt and pepper in a bowl and beat with a whisk to blend.

- Pour the dressing over the salad just before serving and toss to coat.

Serves 4 to 6

Strawberry Spinach Salad

8 cups torn spinach
3 kiwifruit, peeled, sliced
1 cup fresh strawberries, thickly
   sliced
3/4 cup chopped pecans or
   macadamia nuts
2 tablespoons strawberry jam
2 tablespoons balsamic vinegar
1/3 cup vegetable oil

- Toss the spinach, kiwifruit, strawberries and pecans in a large bowl, reserving a few slices of the kiwifruit and strawberries for garnish.

- Process the strawberry jam and balsamic vinegar in a blender until smooth. Add the oil in a fine stream, processing constantly.

- Pour over the spinach mixture and toss gently to coat.

- Garnish with the reserved kiwifruit and strawberry slices.

Serves 4

Garden Greens with Yogurt Dressing

Very good.

1 bunch arugula
1 small bunch French curly lettuce
    or frisée
1 small head Boston lettuce
1/2 cup low-fat plain yogurt
1 1/2 tablespoons light mayonnaise
2 teaspoons honey
2 1/2 teaspoons Dijon mustard
1 1/2 tablespoons fresh lemon juice
1 scallion, minced
Salt and pepper to taste

- Rinse the arugula, curly lettuce and Boston lettuce and spin dry. Tear into bite-sized pieces into a large salad bowl.

- Combine the yogurt, mayonnaise, honey, Dijon mustard, lemon juice, scallion, salt and pepper in a small bowl and beat with a whisk until blended.

- Pour over the salad greens and toss to coat.

Serves 4

Metro Salad

A favorite at Peacock Hill.

Seasoned Mayonnaise:
1/2 cup light mayonnaise
1/4 teaspoon salt
1 tablespoon white wine
1 teaspoon oregano
1/8 teaspoon white pepper

Salad:
3 cups bite-size cooked chicken
2 unpeeled Granny Smith apples,
    cored, cut into pieces
Juice of 1/2 lemon
2 tablespoons chopped fresh
    parsley
Leaf lettuce
3 tablespoons almonds, toasted

- For the seasoned mayonnaise, combine the mayonnaise, salt, white wine, oregano and white pepper in a small bowl and mix well.

- For the salad, mix the chicken, apples, lemon juice and parsley in a bowl. Add the seasoned mayonnaise and toss to mix well.

- Chill, covered, for several hours before serving.

- To serve, line 4 salad plates with lettuce leaves. Divide the salad mixture evenly among the prepared plates. Sprinkle with the almonds.

Serves 4

Peacock's Club Salad

What else can I say—this salad...wow!

Dressing:
1 cup vegetable oil
1/2 cup olive oil
1/2 cup red wine vinegar
2 tablespoons lemon juice
1 garlic clove, minced
1 teaspoon Dijon mustard
1 1/2 teaspoons Worcestershire
    sauce
1 teaspoon salt
1/2 teaspoon pepper

Salad:
1/2 lemon
2 avocados, sliced
1 head Boston lettuce, rinsed, torn
3/4 to 1 cup watercress
1/4 cup chopped green onions
2 cups chopped chilled cooked
    chicken
1 tomato, chopped
3/4 cup shredded Cheddar cheese
6 slices bacon, crisp-cooked,
    crumbled
2 hard-boiled eggs, chopped

- For the dressing, combine the vegetable oil, olive oil, vinegar, 2 tablespoons lemon juice, garlic, Dijon mustard, Worcestershire sauce, salt and pepper in a jar with a tight-fitting lid. Cover and shake to mix well. Chill, covered, until ready to serve.

- For the salad, squeeze the lemon juice over the avocado slices. Combine the lettuce, watercress, green onions, avocados, chicken, tomato, Cheddar cheese, bacon and eggs in a large bowl. Add the dressing and toss lightly to coat.

Serves 4

Chicken Club Salad

Make this salad several hours ahead of serving time. It is so good.

1 head iceberg lettuce, shredded
Salt and pepper to taste
3 hard-cooked eggs, sliced
3 large skinless chicken breasts,
　cooked, chopped
2 tablespoons chopped green
　onions
1 pint cherry tomatoes, cut into
　halves
1 pound bacon, cooked, crumbled
Mayonnaise
1/4 cup freshly grated Parmesan
　cheese
1 cup (4 ounces) shredded Swiss
　cheese or Monterey Jack cheese

- Layer 1/2 of the lettuce in a large glass bowl. Season with salt and pepper.

- Layer the egg slices, chicken, green onions, tomatoes and bacon over the lettuce. Cover with the remaining lettuce.

- Spread enough mayonnaise over the top to cover completely. Sprinkle with the Parmesan cheese and Swiss cheese.

- Cover loosely and chill until ready to serve.

- Note: You may sprinkle with croutons.

Serves 6

Roast Chicken Breasts for Salad

2 large whole chicken breasts
　(1 1/2 pounds or more each)
1 tablespoon vegetable oil
Salt to taste

- Preheat the oven to 400 degrees.

- Arrange the chicken on a small foil-lined baking pan. Brush with the oil. Sprinkle generously with salt.

- Roast on the middle oven rack for 30 to 40 minutes or until a meat thermometer inserted into the thickest portion registers 160 degrees.

- Remove from the oven and cool to room temperature. Remove and discard the skin. Remove the chicken from the bone. Cut each chicken breast into thirds. Use your hands to pull apart each chicken piece and shred into small chunks.

- Continue with your favorite chicken salad recipe.

- Note: You may wrap the chicken in plastic wrap and store in the refrigerator for 2 days.

Makes about 5 cups shredded chicken

Warm Chicken Salad with Balsamic Dressing

1 bunch red leaf lettuce, torn into
    bite-size pieces
1 bunch green leaf lettuce, torn
    into bite-size pieces
1 bunch radicchio, torn into bite-
    size pieces
2 or 3 Belgian endive, torn into
    bite-size pieces
1 large red bell pepper, cut into
    thin strips
4 boneless skinless chicken breasts
3 tablespoons flour
1/2 teaspoon salt
1/2 teaspoon pepper
3 to 4 tablespoons olive oil
1/2 cup sliced scallions
2 tablespoons (or more) balsamic
    vinegar

- Arrange the red leaf lettuce, green leaf lettuce and radicchio in the center of 4 serving plates. Arrange the endive around the edge of each plate. Arrange the bell pepper strips in a spoke design over the lettuce.

- Pound the chicken to evenly flatten. Coat the chicken with a mixture of flour, salt and pepper.

- Sauté the chicken in the olive oil in a skillet for 3 to 4 minutes on each side or until cooked through. Remove the chicken from the skillet, reserving the pan drippings. Cut the chicken into strips. Arrange in a spoke design between the bell pepper strips.

- Add the scallions to the drippings in the skillet. Sauté lightly. Add the balsamic vinegar, stirring to deglaze the skillet. Drizzle over the salads.

Serves 4

Americana Potato Salad

2 pounds new potatoes
2 tablespoons red wine vinegar
1/2 teaspoon salt and pepper
3 hard-cooked eggs, chopped
2 large scallions, thinly sliced
1 small rib celery, chopped
1/4 cup sweet pickles, chopped
1/2 cup mayonnaise
2 tablespoons Dijon mustard
1/4 cup minced fresh parsley

- Scrub the potatoes and place in a large saucepan. Cover with water. Bring to a boil and reduce the heat. Simmer, covered, for 15 to 20 minutes or until the potatoes are tender; drain. Cool slightly. Peel the potatoes and cut into cubes while still warm.

- Layer the potatoes in a medium bowl, sprinkling each layer with the red wine vinegar, salt and pepper. Chill, covered, in the refrigerator.

- Add the hard-cooked eggs, scallions, celery, sweet pickles, mayonnaise, Dijon mustard and parsley to the potato mixture and mix well.

- Chill, covered, until ready to serve or up to 1 day.

Serves 6 to 8

Potato Salad

Use small red potatoes for the best results.

3 pounds red potatoes
1/2 cup chopped fresh chives
1 tablespoon grated onion
1 teaspoon sugar
1 teaspoon salt
1/2 teaspoon white pepper
1/2 cup sour cream
1/2 cup plain low-fat yogurt
2 to 3 tablespoons mayonnaise
2 teaspoons lemon juice
2 teaspoons Dijon mustard

- Cook the potatoes in boiling water to cover in a saucepan for 30 minutes or until tender. Drain and cool. Peel the potatoes and cut into thin slices.

- Combine the chives, onion, sugar, salt, white pepper, sour cream, yogurt, mayonnaise, lemon juice and Dijon mustard in a large bowl and mix well. Add the potato slices and toss gently to coat.

- Chill, covered, for 2 to 3 hours before serving.

- Serve on radicchio leaves and garnish with chopped fresh basil.

Serves 10

Peppercorn Dressing

A salad of romaine, iceberg lettuce and spinach would be excellent with this dressing.

2 cups mayonnaise
3/4 cup milk
1/4 cup freshly grated Parmesan
    cheese
1 or 2 tablespoons freshly ground
    peppercorns
1 tablespoon cider vinegar
1 teaspoon lemon juice
1 teaspoon minced onion
1 teaspoon garlic salt
Dash of Tabasco sauce
Dash of Worcestershire sauce

- Combine the mayonnaise, milk, Parmesan cheese, peppercorns, cider vinegar, lemon juice, onion, garlic salt, Tabasco sauce and Worcestershire sauce in a bowl and whisk until mixed.

- Chill, covered, for 1 to 12 hours before serving.

- Note: Use a blend of peppercorns.

Makes about 3 1/4 cups

Ranch Dressing Mix

7 tablespoons parsley flakes
5 tablespoons instant minced
   onion
4 teaspoons salt
1 teaspoon garlic powder

- Combine the parsley flakes, minced onion, salt and garlic powder in a bowl and mix well. Store in an airtight container in a cool dry place.

- To prepare, combine 2 tablespoons of the mixture with 1 cup mayonnaise and 1 cup buttermilk and mix well.

- Note: Substitute sour cream for the buttermilk to make a dip for vegetables or chips.

Makes about 3/4 cup

Raspberry Vinaigrette

1 cup olive oil
1/2 cup red wine vinegar
1/4 cup water
1/4 cup vegetable oil
2 tablespoons sugar
1 teaspoon freshly cracked
   pepper
1 cup raspberries

- Combine the olive oil, red wine vinegar, water, vegetable oil, sugar, pepper and raspberries in a food processor. Pulse several times to blend well.

- Pour into a bowl or bottle.

- Store, covered, in the refrigerator.

Serves 4

Sandwiches

After he said this,

Paul took some bread and

thanked God for

it before all of them.

He broke off a piece and

began eating.

Acts 27:35
New Century Version

Hot Ham and Cheese Sandwiches

A favorite at Peacock Hill.

1/2 cup (1 stick) butter, softened
1/4 cup horseradish mustard
1/4 cup finely chopped onion
2 tablespoons poppy seeds
8 buns, split
8 slices Swiss cheese
8 slices baked ham
8 slices Muenster cheese

- Preheat the oven to 350 degrees.

- Combine the butter, horseradish mustard, onion and poppy seeds in a bowl and mix well.

- Spread the mustard mixture on the cut sides of the buns. Layer the bottom half of each bun with Swiss cheese, ham and Muenster cheese. Replace the top of the buns.

- Wrap the sandwiches tightly in heavy foil. Arrange on a baking sheet.

- Bake for 20 to 30 minutes or until heated through.

Serves 8

French Loaf Sandwiches

Feed a group with this one—they'll love it.

2 loaves unsliced French or Italian
    bread
8 ounces cream cheese, softened
1 cup (4 ounces) shredded
    Cheddar cheese
3/4 cup sliced green onions or
    chives
1/4 cup mayonnaise
1 tablespoon Worcestershire sauce
1 pound cooked ham, thinly sliced
1 pound roast beef, thinly sliced
12 to 14 thin slices dill pickle

- Cut the bread into halves lengthwise. Hollow out the top and bottom of the loaves, leaving a 1/2-inch shell.

- Combine the cream cheese, Cheddar cheese, green onions, mayonnaise and Worcestershire sauce in a bowl and mix well. Spread over the cut sides of the bread.

- Layer the ham and roast beef on the bottom and top halves of the bread. Arrange the pickles on the bottom halves. Press the bottom and top halves together gently to form sandwiches.

- Wrap in plastic wrap. Chill for 2 hours or longer before serving. Cut into 1 1/2-inch slices to serve.

Serves 12 to 14

Pizzaburgers

Kids and adults will love you for these gems.

1 pound ground beef
1/2 cup chopped onion
1 (6-ounce) can tomato paste
1 teaspoon salt
1 teaspoon oregano
1/4 teaspoon garlic powder
6 bagels, split, toasted
Sliced or shredded mozzarella
   cheese

- Preheat the oven to 350 degrees.

- Brown the ground beef and onion in a skillet, stirring until the ground beef is crumbly; drain. Add the tomato paste, salt, oregano and garlic powder.

- Simmer, uncovered, for 15 minutes.

- Spoon on the split side of the bagel halves. Cover each with mozzarella cheese. Arrange on a baking sheet.

- Bake for 5 minutes or until the mozzarella cheese melts.

Serves 6

Impatience: Waiting in a hurry.

Stromboli Sandwiches

1 pound ground beef
1 tablespoon chopped onion
1 tablespoon chopped green
 bell pepper
1/2 cup ketchup
1/2 cup tomato sauce
2 tablespoons freshly grated
 Parmesan cheese
1/2 teaspoon garlic powder
1/2 teaspoon oregano
1/4 teaspoon fennel seeds
2 tablespoons butter
1/4 teaspoon garlic powder
4 to 6 buns
Shredded mozzarella cheese

- Preheat the oven to 350 degrees.

- Brown the ground beef in a skillet, stirring until crumbly. Stir in the onion and bell pepper. Add the ketchup, tomato sauce, Parmesan cheese, garlic powder, oregano and fennel seeds and mix well.

- Simmer for 20 minutes.

- Mix the butter and garlic powder in a bowl until smooth.

- Split the buns into halves. Spread the cut side of the top halves with the butter mixture. Spoon the ground beef mixture over the bottom halves of the buns. Sprinkle with mozzarella cheese. Replace the top halves.

- Wrap each sandwich in foil.

- Bake for 15 minutes.

Serves 4 to 6

Barbecued Chicken Sandwiches

4 pounds chicken
1 1/4 cups ketchup
2 cups water
1 onion, finely chopped
1 teaspoon salt
1 teaspoon celery seeds
1 teaspoon chili powder
1/4 cup packed light brown sugar
1/4 cup Tabasco sauce
1/4 cup Worcestershire sauce
1/4 cup red wine vinegar
6 buns

- Place the chicken in a large stockpot and cover with water. Bring to a boil and reduce the heat. Simmer for 1 hour or until the chicken is tender. Drain and cool.

- Shred the chicken, discarding the skin and bones.

- Combine the ketchup, 2 cups water, onion, salt, celery seeds, chili powder, brown sugar, Tabasco sauce, Worcestershire sauce and vinegar in a large saucepan and mix well. Add the shredded chicken and mix well.

- Simmer for 1 1/2 hours.

- Split the buns into halves. Spoon the chicken mixture onto the bottom halves of the buns. Replace the top halves.

Serves 6

Original 1850s farmhouse before renovation in 1994.

Turkey Avocado Sandwiches

Wonderful "dressed-up" sandwich. Enjoy!

Butter
Dijon mustard
Black pepper
Dash of cayenne pepper
4 thick slices whole wheat bread
4 slices turkey breast
1/2 red onion, sliced, separated
    into rings
4 thin slices Swiss cheese
1 tablespoon balsamic vinegar
1 tablespoon olive oil
1/8 teaspoon cayenne pepper
2 ripe avocados, sliced
Bean sprouts or chopped lettuce

- Preheat the broiler.

- Combine butter, Dijon mustard, black pepper and a dash of cayenne pepper in a bowl and mix well. Spread on the bread slices.

- Top each bread slice with turkey, red onion and Swiss cheese. Arrange on a baking sheet.

- Broil until the cheese is melted and the sandwiches are heated through.

- Mix the balsamic vinegar, olive oil and 1/8 teaspoon cayenne pepper in a small bowl. Add the avocado slices and turn to coat.

- Top each sandwich with avocado slices and a mound of bean sprouts.

Serves 4

Lord make my words soft and tender,
for tomorrow I may have to eat them.

Tea Sandwiches

Honey Mustard Butter:

1/2 cup (1 stick) butter, softened
1/4 cup honey
2 teaspoons prepared mustard

Cranberry Butter:

1 cup sugar
1/2 cup water
1 1/4 cups cranberries
1/2 cup (1 stick) butter, softened
1 tablespoon confectioners' sugar

Sandwiches:

1 recipe Yogurt Crescent Rolls
    (page 27)
1 pound thinly sliced turkey,
    cut into 2-inch squares

- For the honey mustard butter, beat 1/2 cup butter, honey and mustard in a mixing bowl until light and fluffy.

- For the cranberry butter, bring the sugar and water to a boil in a small saucepan over medium heat, stirring until the sugar dissolves. Stir in the cranberries. Bring to a boil and reduce the heat. Simmer for 10 to 15 minutes or until thickened, stirring occasionally. Remove from the heat and cool completely.

- Press through a fine mesh strainer, discarding the solids. Beat 1/2 cup butter at medium speed in a mixing bowl until light and fluffy. Add the confectioners' sugar and cranberry mixture and beat until smooth.

- For the sandwiches, prepare the roll recipe, cutting the dough into small circles instead of crescents. Bake according to the recipe instructions. Cut the rolls into halves. Spread the cut sides of the rolls evenly with the honey mustard butter or the cranberry butter. Arrange the turkey evenly over the bottom halves. Replace the tops.

Makes 50 sandwiches

Entrées

Everything that moves,

everything that is alive,

is yours for food.

Earlier I gave you the green

plants, but now

I give you everything

for food.

Genesis 9:3
New Century Version

Rosemary Chicken and Veggies

Real comfort and real good.

1 (3-pound) chicken
1 garlic clove, minced
1 tablespoon olive oil
4 medium red potatoes, cut into
    quarters
5 medium carrots, cut into thirds
3 ribs celery, cut into 2-inch pieces
2 medium onions, cut into wedges
1 cup chicken broth
1/3 cup dry white wine
1 tablespoon chopped fresh
    rosemary, or 1 teaspoon dried
    rosemary
1/4 teaspoon salt
1/4 teaspoon pepper
1 tablespoon cornstarch
2 tablespoons cold water

- Cut the chicken into pieces and remove the skin.

- Sauté the garlic in the olive oil in a skillet. Add the chicken. Cook for 10 minutes or until light brown; drain.

- Add the red potatoes, carrots, celery, onions, broth, wine, rosemary, salt and pepper. Bring to a boil and reduce the heat.

- Simmer, covered, for 35 minutes or until the chicken is cooked through and tender. Remove the chicken and vegetables to a serving platter, reserving the drippings in the skillet.

- Dissolve the cornstarch in the water in a bowl. Add to the reserved drippings in the skillet. Cook until thickened, stirring constantly. Serve over the chicken.

Serves 4 to 6

Country Chicken with Angel Biscuits

1 (3-pound) chicken, cut up
2 teaspoons salt
1 rib celery
1 medium onion, cut into quarters
5 carrots, cut into pieces
1/4 cup (1/2 stick) butter
6 tablespoons flour
1 cup half-and-half
2 egg yolks, beaten
Angel Biscuits (page 35)

- Place the chicken in a saucepan and cover with water. Season with the salt. Add the celery and onion. Simmer, covered, until the chicken is cooked through and tender. Drain the chicken, reserving the broth. Cook the carrots in a small amount of water in a saucepan for 10 minutes.

- Melt the butter in a saucepan. Stir in the flour. Cook for 2 minutes. Stir in 2 cups of the reserved broth and half-and-half gradually. Cook until smooth and thickened, stirring constantly with a whisk and adding enough of the remaining broth as needed for the desired consistency.

- Add a small amount of the hot sauce to the egg yolks in a bowl. Add the egg yolks to the hot sauce. Cook for 2 minutes, stirring constantly.

- Arrange the chicken and carrots in a serving dish. Cover with the sauce. Top with Angel Biscuits. Have a basket handy for the extra Angel Biscuits.

Serves 4 to 6

Champagne Chicken

6 boneless skinless chicken breasts
3 tablespoons lemon juice
Pepper to taste
2 tablespoons butter
1 tablespoon olive oil
2 tablespoons butter
1/4 cup chopped shallots
2 medium garlic cloves, minced
3/4 cup chicken stock
3/4 cup Champagne
3 tablespoons lemon juice
1 1/4 cups heavy cream
2 tablespoons minced chives

- Pound each chicken breast to an even thickness. Sprinkle with 3 tablespoons lemon juice and pepper, allowing 1/2 teaspoon lemon juice per chicken breast.

- Melt 2 tablespoons butter in a large skillet. Stir in the olive oil. Add the chicken. Cook over medium-high heat for 2 minutes per side or until brown. Remove to a platter, reserving the pan drippings in the skillet. Cover and keep warm. Melt 2 tablespoons butter in the reserved pan drippings. Add the shallots. Sauté until translucent. Add the garlic. Cook for 2 minutes, stirring to deglaze the skillet.

- Add the chicken stock, Champagne and 3 tablespoons lemon juice. Bring to a boil and reduce the heat. Simmer until the sauce is reduced to a glaze consistency.

- Add the cream. Boil for 6 minutes or until thickened, stirring constantly. Return the chicken to the skillet. Cook until heated through. Sprinkle with the chives.

Serves 6

*Hospitality is making your guests feel at home—
even when you wish they were.*

Chicken Breasts and Mushrooms with Rosemary and Mustard Sauce

Wonderful entrée for spring and summer guests. Serve with mashed potatoes or angel hair pasta.

2 tablespoons butter
6 boneless skinless chicken
    breasts
Salt and pepper to taste
1 tablespoon butter
6 green onions, sliced
2 cups sliced mushrooms
3/4 cup dry white wine
1 cup chicken broth
1/4 teaspoon salt
1 tablespoon chopped fresh
    rosemary, or 3/4 teaspoon
    dried rosemary
2 tablespoons Dijon mustard
2 tablespoons chopped fresh
    parsley

- Melt 2 tablespoons butter in a skillet over medium heat. Season the chicken with salt and pepper to taste. Add to the skillet. Cook for 20 minutes or until brown. Remove the chicken to a plate and keep warm.

- Add 1 tablespoon butter, the green onions and mushrooms to the skillet. Sauté until the mushrooms are tender. Remove with a slotted spoon to the plate with the chicken.

- Add the wine, broth, 1/4 teaspoon salt and rosemary to the drippings in the skillet. Increase the heat. Boil for 5 minutes or until the liquid is reduced by 1/2. Add the Dijon mustard and parsley and stir with a whisk.

- Return the chicken and mushroom mixture to the skillet. Simmer for 5 to 10 minutes or until the chicken is cooked through.

- Garnish with fresh rosemary sprigs and serve immediately.

Serves 4

Love is the specialty of the House.

Chicken Breasts Marsala

Angel hair pasta makes a nice side.

6 boneless skinless chicken breasts
Salt and pepper to taste
1/2 cup flour
1 cup (2 sticks) butter or olive oil
3/4 cup marsala
1/2 cup chicken broth
1/4 cup (1/2 stick) butter or olive oil
1/2 cup sliced mushrooms
1/2 cup grated Parmesan cheese
1/2 cup (2 ounces) shredded
    mozzarella cheese

- Preheat the oven to 400 degrees. Pound the chicken breasts to flatten. Season with salt and pepper. Dredge in the flour. Melt 1 cup butter in a skillet over medium heat. Add the chicken.

- Sauté for 3 to 4 minutes on each side or until light brown. Arrange the chicken in a 9×13-inch baking dish, reserving the drippings in the skillet. Add the wine and chicken broth to the reserved drippings, stirring to deglaze the skillet. Simmer for 10 minutes.

- Melt 1/4 cup butter in a skillet over medium heat. Add the mushrooms. Sauté until tender. Spoon over the chicken. Mix the Parmesan cheese and mozzarella cheese in a bowl. Sprinkle over the mushrooms. Pour the wine sauce over the top.

- Bake for 10 to 12 minutes or until heated through. Broil for 2 minutes or until the top is light brown.

Serves 6

Orange Hazelnut Chicken

Delicious served with mashed potatoes.

1 cup fine dry bread crumbs
1/4 cup finely chopped toasted
    hazelnuts or almonds
3 tablespoons chopped fresh
    parsley
1/2 teaspoon thyme
1/2 teaspoon salt
1/8 teaspoon pepper
2 tablespoons butter
1/4 cup fresh orange juice
4 to 6 boneless skinless chicken
    breasts

- Preheat the oven to 350 degrees.

- Mix the bread crumbs, hazelnuts, parsley, thyme, salt and pepper together. Melt the butter in a saucepan. Add the orange juice and mix well.

- Dip the chicken in the butter mixture; roll in the crumb mixture. Arrange in a 7×11-inch baking dish sprayed with nonstick cooking spray. Pour the remaining butter mixture over the chicken.

- Bake, uncovered, for 35 minutes or until the chicken is cooked through. Garnish as desired.

Serves 4

White Sherry Chicken

A great dish to serve for company.

3/4 cup plain bread crumbs
3/4 cup Italian bread crumbs
1/4 cup grated Parmesan cheese
Freshly ground pepper to taste
1 cup (2 sticks) unsalted butter
12 chicken breasts
1 cup (2 sticks) unsalted butter
1 cup white sherry
1 (10-ounce) jar orange
  marmalade

- Mix the bread crumbs, Parmesan cheese and pepper in a large bowl. Melt 1 cup butter in a shallow dish. Dip the chicken in the hot melted butter to coat. Roll in the bread crumb mixture to coat thoroughly. Arrange on a well-greased baking sheet. Chill, covered, for at least 2 hours to set.

- Preheat the oven to 350 degrees.

- Melt 1 cup butter in a medium saucepan. Bring almost to a rolling boil. Add the sherry all at once. Cook for a few minutes or until the mixture is reduced, stirring frequently. Add the orange marmalade and mix well. Season with pepper. Bring to a slow boil. Cook for 10 to 15 minutes. Reduce the heat to low to keep warm.

- Remove the baking sheet from the refrigerator and place immediately into the oven. Bake for 45 minutes, basting with the orange mixture every 8 minutes. Turn off the oven. Let the chicken stand in the oven for 5 minutes or until the last baste has set. Serve with hot cooked rice.

Serves 12

Escalloped Chicken

An excellent "chicken and dressing" recipe. Great to serve for Thanksgiving or Christmas dinner.

3 pounds skinless chicken breasts
1 1/2 cups chopped celery
1 1/2 cups chopped onion
6 to 8 tablespoons butter
8 cups corn bread, crumbled
1/2 teaspoon poultry seasoning
1/2 teaspoon sage
1/2 teaspoon pepper
1/4 cup (1/2 stick) butter
6 tablespoons flour
1 1/2 cups skim milk
Pinch of salt
3 eggs, beaten
Breadcrumbs

- Preheat the oven to 300 degrees.

- Place the chicken in a large saucepan and cover with water. Cook until the chicken is cooked through. Drain the chicken, reserving the broth. Cut the chicken into pieces, discarding the bones.

- Sauté the celery and onion in 6 to 8 tablespoons butter in a small skillet until tender. Combine the corn bread, sautéed vegetable mixture, poultry seasoning, sage and pepper in a large bowl and mix well. Add enough of the reserved broth to moisten.

- Spoon into a greased 9×13-inch baking dish, pressing down firmly.

- Melt 1/4 cup butter in a saucepan. Add the flour and stir to form a paste. Stir in the milk and salt. Cook until thickened, stirring constantly. Add a small amount of the hot mixture to the beaten eggs in a bowl; add the eggs to the hot mixture and stir to mix well. Remove from the heat to cool.

- Layer 1/2 of the sauce over the dressing. Arrange the chicken over the sauce. Cover with the remaining sauce. Sprinkle with bread crumbs and press down. Bake for 1 1/2 hours.

- Note: This can be made the night before and refrigerated. It is actually much better made the day before serving.

Serves 12

Chicken Piccata

Simplicity impresses most people. Don't overcook the chicken.

Flour
Garlic powder to taste
Salt and pepper to taste
4 boneless skinless chicken breasts
1/4 cup (1/2 stick) butter
Juice of 2 lemons
3 ounces drained capers
1/4 cup chopped fresh parsley

- Mix the flour, garlic powder, salt and pepper together. Pound the chicken to flatten slightly. Dredge in the flour mixture.

- Melt the butter in a skillet. Add the chicken. Cook until the chicken is brown. Pour the lemon juice over the chicken. Reduce the heat. Cook, covered, for 8 to 10 minutes or until the chicken is cooked through. Add the capers and parsley. Cook until heated through, stirring and basting the chicken with the pan juices.

- Garnish with fresh lemon slices. Serve with Almond Rice (page 133).

Serves 4

Creamed Chicken

Delicious served over Almond Rice on page 133.

4 boneless skinless chicken breasts
6 tablespoons butter
1/2 medium onion, minced
12 ounces mushrooms, sliced
1 cup heavy cream or milk
3/4 cup grated Parmesan cheese
Salt and white pepper to taste

- Cut the chicken into strips. Sauté in the butter in a skillet for 3 to 5 minutes or until the chicken is cooked through. Add the onion and mushrooms. Sauté for 3 to 4 minutes or until the onion is translucent.

- Add the cream. Cook over medium heat until the sauce is the desired consistency. Stir in the cheese. Season with salt and white pepper.

Serves 4

Chicken and Zucchini with Angel Hair Pasta

Super good.

5 small zucchini, julienned
1/4 teaspoon salt
1/4 cup plus 1 tablespoon olive oil
2 boneless skinless chicken breasts,
  cut into 1-inch pieces
1 1/2 cups chopped onions
1 garlic clove, minced
2/3 cup whipping cream
1/2 cup grated Parmesan cheese
1/4 teaspoon salt
1/8 teaspoon pepper
7 cups drained cooked angel hair
  pasta
1/4 cup grated Parmesan cheese

- Sauté the zucchini and 1/4 teaspoon salt in the olive oil in a large skillet until tender. Remove from the skillet and drain on paper towels.

- Add the chicken, onions and garlic to the skillet. Cook over medium heat for 8 minutes or until the chicken is tender. Stir in the whipping cream. Bring to a boil and reduce the heat. Simmer for 5 minutes or until the sauce is reduced by 1/3. Add the sautéed zucchini, 1/2 cup Parmesan cheese, 1/4 teaspoon salt, pepper and cooked pasta and mix well. Cook until heated through. Sprinkle with 1/4 cup Parmesan cheese.

- Serve in individual heated serving bowls. This makes it easier to eat and retains the heat longer.

- Note: You may substitute fettuccini for the angel hair pasta and add sliced fresh mushrooms.

Serves 8

Italian Chicken Fettuccini

A great supper dish.

8 ounces uncooked fettuccini
4 boneless skinless chicken breasts
1 cup sliced mushrooms
1 cup (or less) minced onion
1 tablespoon butter
1 cup dry white wine
1 cup whipping cream
1 tablespoon butter
1/4 teaspoon salt
1/4 teaspoon pepper
1/4 teaspoon garlic powder, or
  1 garlic clove, minced
1/2 cup grated Parmesan cheese
2 cups (8 ounces) shredded
  mozzarella cheese

- Preheat the oven to 350 degrees. Cook the pasta using the package directions; drain. Rinse in cold water and drain well.

- Cut the chicken into strips. Sauté the chicken, mushrooms and onion in 1 tablespoon butter in a large skillet until the chicken is tender and light brown. Add the wine and mix well. Simmer, covered, until almost dry.

- Scald the whipping cream in a small saucepan. Add 1 tablespoon butter, salt, pepper and garlic powder. Heat until the butter melts, stirring constantly. Arrange the pasta in a 1-quart baking dish. Sprinkle with the Parmesan cheese. Pour the cream mixture over the pasta. Add the chicken mixture. Sprinkle with the mozzarella cheese.

- Bake for 20 minutes or until the mozzarella cheese is bubbly and light brown.

Serves 4

Chicken Linguini

A very good and tasty dish.

4 boneless skinless chicken breasts
2 sprigs of fresh parsley
1/4 teaspoon salt
1 tablespoon olive oil
1/2 cup chopped onion
2 garlic cloves, minced
4 to 6 mushrooms, sliced
2 tomatoes, seeded, chopped
1/4 cup fresh basil leaves, chopped,
    or 1 teaspoon dried basil
1/4 teaspoon salt
Pepper to taste
12 ounces linguini, cooked,
    drained
Freshly grated Parmesan cheese

- Place the chicken in a saucepan and add the parsley and 1/4 teaspoon salt. Cover with water. Bring to a boil and reduce the heat. Simmer for 15 to 25 minutes or until the chicken is cooked through. Drain, discarding the parsley. Let the chicken stand until cool. Cut into 1/2-inch strips.

- Heat the olive oil in a saucepan over medium heat. Add the onion, garlic and mushrooms. Sauté for 5 minutes or until the vegetables are tender. Add the chicken, tomatoes, basil, 1/4 teaspoon salt and pepper. Simmer for 5 minutes or until heated through.

- Pour over the cooked pasta in a large serving bowl and toss to coat. Sprinkle with Parmesan cheese and serve immediately.

Serves 4

Chicken Tetrazzini

The best casserole.

4 large boneless skinless chicken
    breasts
1 1/2 cups chopped celery
1 medium onion, chopped
8 ounces sliced mushrooms
5 tablespoons butter
1/4 cup flour
2 teaspoons salt
1/4 teaspoon pepper
1 cup whipping cream
2 1/2 tablespoons dry sherry
8 ounces angel hair pasta, cooked,
    drained
3/4 cup bread crumbs
5 tablespoons grated Parmesan
    cheese
Butter for topping

- Preheat the oven to 350 degrees.

- Cook the chicken in water to cover in a saucepan until cooked through. Drain the chicken, reserving 2 cups broth. Cut the chicken into bite-size pieces.

- Sauté the celery, onion and mushrooms in 5 tablespoons butter in a saucepan until the vegetables are tender. Add the flour, salt and pepper. Add the reserved chicken broth and whipping cream gradually. Cook until thickened, stirring constantly. Add the chicken and sherry and mix well.

- Arrange the pasta in a greased 9×13-inch baking dish. Pour the chicken mixture over the pasta. Sprinkle with the bread crumbs and Parmesan cheese. Dot with butter.

- Bake for 30 minutes or until light brown and bubbly.

Serves 6 to 8

Polenta with Rosemary and Walnuts

So good.

2 1/2 cups chicken broth
2/3 cup yellow cornmeal
3/4 cup grated Gruyère cheese
1 1/2 tablespoons butter
1/3 cup finely chopped toasted
   walnuts
1 1/2 teaspoons chopped fresh
   rosemary, or 1/2 teaspoon dried
   rosemary
Salt and pepper to taste
1 1/2 tablespoons butter
Walnut halves

- Preheat the oven to 350 degrees.

- Bring the chicken broth to a boil in a heavy saucepan. Add the cornmeal gradually, stirring with a whisk. Reduce the heat. Cook for 6 minutes or until thickened, whisking constantly. Remove from the heat.

- Add the cheese and 1 1/2 tablespoons butter and stir until the cheese melts. Stir in the chopped walnuts and rosemary. Season with salt and pepper.

- Spoon into a buttered 9-inch glass pie plate and spread evenly with a buttered knife. Cool until firm. You may cover and refrigerate until the next day.

- Cut the polenta into 8 wedges. Arrange the wedges bottom side up on a foil-lined baking sheet. Dot with 1 1/2 tablespoons butter. Arrange a walnut half in the center of each wedge.

- Bake for 12 minutes or until heated through.

Serves 8

Beef Fillets with Balsamic Sauce

Beef:
4 (6-ounce) beef fillets
2 tablespoons kosher salt
1 tablespoon ground pepper
2 tablespoons olive oil

Balsamic Sauce:
1/4 cup dry red wine
1/4 cup dry sherry
3 tablespoons balsamic vinegar
1 shallot, chopped
2 garlic cloves, chopped
2 egg yolks
1/3 cup unsalted butter, melted

- Preheat the oven to 350 degrees.

- For the beef, rub the beef with the kosher salt and pepper.

- Cook the beef in the olive oil in a large ovenproof skillet over high heat for 2 to 3 minutes on each side.

- Bake for 8 to 15 minutes or to the desired degree of doneness. Remove to a serving platter.

- For the balsamic sauce, bring the red wine, sherry, balsamic vinegar, shallot and garlic to a boil in a small saucepan. Cook for 2 minutes. Remove from the heat to cool.

- Whisk the egg yolks into the cooled mixture. Cook over low heat until thickened, whisking constantly. Whisk in the butter gradually and blend well.

- To serve, spoon the balsamic sauce over the beef.

Serves 4

Never let the opportunity to say a kind word pass.

Barbecued Round Steak

2 pounds round steak, cut into
    2-inch pieces
Vegetable oil for browning
1 cup chopped onion
1 teaspoon vegetable oil
1/2 cup white wine vinegar
1/4 cup chili sauce
1/4 cup tomato sauce
2 teaspoons chili powder
2 teaspoons Worcestershire sauce
2 teaspoons sugar
1/4 teaspoon thyme
1 cup stewed tomatoes
1/2 cup beef broth
1/2 cup red wine
8 buns, toasted

- Preheat the oven to 300 degrees.

- Brown the beef in a small amount of oil in a large skillet. Arrange in a baking dish.

- Sauté the onion in 1 teaspoon oil in a skillet for 3 minutes. Add the vinegar, chili sauce, tomato sauce, chili powder, Worcestershire sauce, sugar, thyme, tomatoes, beef broth and wine and mix well. Bring to a boil. Pour over the beef.

- Bake, covered, for 1 1/2 hours or until the beef falls apart in shreds when pierced with a fork. Shred the beef and mix with the sauce.

- Spoon over the toasted buns.

Serves 8

Asian Beef and Pasta

1 pound beef sirloin, cut 1/2 inch
    thick
1 tablespoon olive oil
1/2 teaspoon garlic powder
1/4 cup crunchy peanut butter
1/4 cup soy sauce
2 tablespoons dark sesame oil
1/4 cup rice wine vinegar
2 tablespoons water
2 teaspoons sugar
1/2 teaspoon garlic powder
1/4 teaspoon pepper
4 large green onions, sliced
4 cups drained hot cooked angel
    hair pasta or fettuccini
1 tablespoon sesame seeds, toasted
2 tablespoons chopped fresh parsley

- Cut the beef crosswise into 1/8×2-inch strips.

- Heat the olive oil in a medium skillet. Add the beef strips and 1/2 teaspoon garlic powder. Stir-fry for 5 minutes or until the beef is the desired degree of doneness. Remove from the heat and keep warm.

- Combine the peanut butter, soy sauce, sesame oil, rice wine vinegar, water, sugar, 1/2 teaspoon garlic powder and pepper in a large bowl and whisk to blend well. Stir in the green onions.

- Add the hot pasta and beef and toss to mix well. Sprinkle with sesame seeds and parsley.

- Garnish with red bell pepper strips.

Serves 4

Chuckwagon Beef Stew

1 pound beef round, cut into
    3/4-inch cubes
Salt and pepper to taste
1 tablespoon hot garlic oil or
    vegetable oil
1 large onion, chopped
1 garlic clove, minced
2 teaspoons Worcestershire sauce
1/2 teaspoon marjoram
1/4 teaspoon cayenne pepper
    (optional)
1 bay leaf
1 pound red potatoes, cut into
    1-inch pieces
2 large carrots, thickly sliced
4 ounces green beans, cut into
    1-inch lengths

- Season the beef lightly with salt and pepper.

- Heat the garlic oil in a heavy Dutch oven over medium heat. Add the beef. Cook for 5 to 7 minutes or until brown, stirring occasionally. Remove with a slotted spoon to a warm platter to keep warm.

- Add the onion to the Dutch oven. Cook for 5 to 7 minutes. Add the garlic. Cook for 1 minute.

- Return the beef to the Dutch oven. Add the Worcestershire sauce, marjoram, cayenne pepper, bay leaf and enough water to barely cover. Simmer, covered, for 30 minutes.

- Add the potatoes and carrots. Simmer, covered, for 10 minutes, stirring once or twice. Add the green beans. Simmer for 5 to 10 minutes or until the beef and vegetables are tender.

- Remove 1/2 cup of the potatoes and carrots and 1/2 cup of the liquid to a blender. Process until puréed. Return to the Dutch oven. Cook until slightly thickened, stirring frequently. Season with salt and pepper. Discard the bay leaf before serving.

Serves 4

Mexicali Beef Cubes

1/4 cup flour
2 teaspoons salt
1/2 teaspoon pepper
2 1/2 to 3 pounds beef, trimmed,
    cut into cubes
1/4 cup shortening
2 garlic cloves, minced
1 cup water
1 cup beef broth
2 medium onions, sliced
6 to 8 red potatoes, peeled, cut
    into cubes
6 carrots, sliced
1 (10-ounce) can diced tomatoes
    with green chiles
1/4 cup chopped fresh parsley
Salt and pepper to taste

- Preheat the oven to 325 degrees.

- Combine the flour, 2 teaspoons salt and 1/2 teaspoon pepper in a sealable plastic bag and shake to mix well. Add the beef cubes a few at a time and shake to coat.

- Melt the shortening in a 4-quart Dutch oven. Add the beef and garlic. Cook until the beef is brown. Add the water, beef broth and onions.

- Bake, covered, for 1 1/4 hours.

- Cook the potatoes and carrots in water to cover in a saucepan until tender; drain.

- Add the potatoes and carrots, tomatoes with green chiles and parsley to the beef mixture just before serving and stir to mix well. Season with salt and pepper to taste.

- Serve with French Bread (page 30).

Serves 6 to 8

Beef Olé

Another favorite recipe of the family. You can add hot peppers, salsa, etc., whatever you like.

1 pound ground beef
1 onion, chopped
1 green bell pepper, chopped
1 (6-ounce) can tomato paste
1 cup water
1/2 teaspoon paprika
1 teaspoon oregano
1 teaspoon garlic powder
Kosher salt and pepper to taste
1 cup (4 ounces) shredded
    Cheddar cheese
2 tomatoes, sliced, cut into
    quarters
1/2 head of lettuce, shredded
Corn chips

- Brown the ground beef and onion in a heavy skillet over medium heat; drain. Stir in the bell pepper, tomato paste, water, paprika, oregano, garlic powder, kosher salt and pepper.

- Bring to a boil. Cover and reduce the heat. Simmer for 25 minutes.

- Place the cheese, tomatoes and lettuce in separate bowls.

- To serve, spread some corn chips on each serving plate. Spoon some of the ground beef mixture over the chips. Top with the cheese, tomatoes and lettuce.

Serves 4

Baked Ground Beef and Zucchini

Very good supper dish.

1 pound ground round
2 onions, chopped
1 (16-ounce) can tomatoes,
    drained
1 (16-ounce) can tomato sauce
3 tablespoons chopped green bell
    pepper
2 ounces mozzarella cheese,
    shredded (1/2 cup)
1/2 teaspoon oregano
1/4 teaspoon garlic powder
1/4 teaspoon salt
1/4 teaspoon pepper
4 medium zucchini, cut into
    1/4-inch slices
1 ounce Parmesan cheese,
    shredded (1/2 cup)

- Preheat the oven to 350 degrees.

- Brown the ground round and onions in a large skillet over low heat, stirring until the ground round is crumbly and the onion is tender; drain. Add the tomatoes, tomato sauce and bell pepper.

- Cook over medium heat for 10 minutes, stirring occasionally. Stir in the mozzarella cheese, oregano, garlic powder, salt and pepper. Add the zucchini.

- Simmer for 10 minutes. Pour into an ungreased 9-inch baking dish. Sprinkle with the Parmesan cheese.

- Bake for 45 minutes.

Serves 6

Sloppy Chen

Quick, easy and delicious.

2 tablespoons vegetable oil
1 medium onion, chopped
1 pound lean ground beef
2 cups sliced mushrooms
3 tablespoons Szechuan stir-fry
    sauce
1 teaspoon cornstarch
3 tablespoons cold water

- Heat the oil in a wok or skillet over medium heat. Add the onion. Sauté until light brown. Add the ground beef. Sauté until the ground beef is brown and crumbly. Stir in the mushrooms. Sauté for 30 seconds.

- Add the stir-fry sauce. Stir-fry until heated through.

- Mix the cornstarch and water in a small bowl. Add to the ground beef mixture. Cook until the sauce is slightly thickened, stirring constantly.

- Serve over hot cooked rice.

Serves 3 or 4

Stove-Top Meat Loaf

A family favorite used for years. It came from the label on the Campbell's soup can.

1 (10-ounce) can Campbell's
    tomato rice soup
1 1/2 pounds ground beef
1/2 cup fine dry bread crumbs
1 egg, lightly beaten
1/4 cup finely chopped onion
1 teaspoon kosher salt
Shortening for browning
1/3 cup water

- Combine 1/4 cup of the soup, ground beef, bread crumbs, egg, onion and kosher salt in a large bowl and mix well. Shape firmly into 2 loaves.

- Brown the loaves on all sides in a small amount of shortening in a skillet over medium-high heat. Simmer, covered, for 25 minutes; drain.

- Pour a mixture of the remaining soup and water over the loaves. Cook, uncovered, for 10 minutes, stirring and basting frequently.

Serves 6

Three-Cheese Italiano

Great Italian flavor.

Crust:
6 ounces angel hair pasta, cooked,
    drained
1/2 garlic clove, minced
1/4 cup (1/2 stick) butter, melted
1/2 cup grated Parmesan cheese
1 egg, beaten
1 tablespoon chopped fresh basil,
    or 1 teaspoon dried basil

Filling:
1 1/4 pounds ground beef
1/2 cup chopped onion
1 (14-ounce) can crushed
    tomatoes
1 (6-ounce) can tomato paste
1 teaspoon sugar
1 teaspoon oregano
1 teaspoon basil
1/4 cup white wine

Assembly:
1 cup ricotta cheese
6 ounces mozzarella cheese,
    shredded (1 1/2 cups)

- Preheat the oven to 350 degrees.

- For the crust, combine the pasta, garlic, butter, Parmesan cheese, egg and 1 tablespoon basil in a bowl and mix well. Cut through the mixture with a knife to chop. Press into a 10-inch pie plate or make individual pies using small tart dishes or pans.

- For the filling, brown the ground beef and onion in a skillet, stirring until the ground beef is crumbly; drain. Add the tomatoes, tomato paste, sugar, oregano, 1 teaspoon basil and wine and mix well. Cook until heated through, stirring frequently.

- To assemble, spread the ricotta cheese over the crust. Spoon in the filling.

- Bake for 20 minutes. Sprinkle with the mozzarella cheese. Bake for 5 minutes longer.

Serves 6 to 8

Pork Medallions with Creamy Apple and Sage Sauce

Tastes great in the fall when fresh cider is made and apples are at their peak.

2 pork tenderloins (2 pounds or
    more)
Salt and pepper to taste
Flour for coating
1 tablespoon unsalted butter
2 Granny Smith apples, peeled,
    cored, cut into 12 slices
5 shallots, thinly sliced
1/2 medium onion, thinly sliced
1/3 cup apple cider
3 tablespoons applejack or brandy
1/2 cup chicken broth
2 tablespoons minced fresh sage
1/4 cup heavy cream

- Trim the pork and cut into 3/4-inch medallions. Season with salt and pepper. Add to flour in a sealable plastic bag and shake to coat. Cook in a nonstick skillet over medium-high heat until brown and cooked through. Remove to a warm platter and cover to keep warm.

- Add the butter to the skillet and heat until melted. Add the apples, shallots and onion. Sauté for 4 minutes or until the apples begin to brown. Add the cider and applejack. Boil for 2 1/2 minutes or until the liquid reduces to a glaze consistency.

- Increase the heat to high. Add the broth, sage and any accumulated pork juices. Boil for 3 minutes or until the liquid is reduced to the consistency of maple syrup. Add the cream. Boil for 2 minutes or until the liquid is reduced by 1/2.

- Reduce the heat to medium. Return the pork to the skillet, turning to coat. Simmer for 3 minutes or until the pork is heated through. Adjust the seasonings to taste.

- Remove the pork to a serving platter. Spoon the sauce over the top. Serve immediately with Overnight Mashed Potatoes (page 121).

Serves 4

Pork Tenderloins with Cranberry Port Sauce

Cranberry Port Sauce:
3 tablespoons butter
2 cups chopped onions
4 garlic cloves, minced
1 1/2 teaspoons grated orange zest
1 1/2 teaspoons sage
1 teaspoon thyme
2 cups chicken broth
1 1/2 cups cranberry juice
2 cups fresh or frozen cranberries
1/2 cup sugar
1/4 cup tawny port
1 tablespoon cornstarch
Salt and pepper to taste

Pork:
4 1/2 teaspoons thyme
1 1/2 teaspoons salt
1 1/2 teaspoons pepper
3 (1-pound) pork tenderloins,
    trimmed
3 tablespoons canola oil
1 1/2 teaspoons grated orange zest

- For the sauce, melt the butter in a large heavy skillet over medium-high heat. Add the onions. Sauté for 8 minutes or until golden brown.

- Add the garlic, 1 1/2 teaspoons orange zest, sage and 1 teaspoon thyme. Cook for 1 minute, stirring constantly. Add the broth and cranberry juice. Simmer for 8 minutes or until the mixture is reduced to 2 1/2 cups.

- Strain the sauce into a medium heavy saucepan, pressing on the solids with the back of a spoon to extract the liquid. Add the cranberries and sugar. Boil for 5 minutes or until the cranberries pop.

- Mix the port and cornstarch in a small bowl until blended. Add to the sauce. Boil for 1 minute or until thickened, stirring constantly. Season with salt and pepper to taste. The cranberry sauce can be made a day ahead and stored, covered, in the refrigerator.

- For the pork, mix 4 1/2 teaspoons thyme, 1 1/2 teaspoons salt and 1 1/2 teaspoons pepper in a small bowl.

- Arrange the pork in a large baking dish. Pat dry with paper towels. Brush with 2 tablespoons of the canola oil. Rub the thyme mixture over the pork. The pork can be prepared a day ahead and stored, covered, in the refrigerator.

- Preheat the oven to 400 degrees.

- Heat the remaining 1 tablespoon canola oil in a heavy large ovenproof skillet over high heat. Add the pork. Cook for 5 minutes or until brown, turning frequently. Place in the oven. Bake for 20 minutes or until a thermometer inserted into the thickest portion registers 150 degrees. Remove the pork to a platter. Cover and keep warm.

- Add the sauce and 1 1/2 teaspoons orange zest to the drippings in the skillet. Bring to a simmer, stirring frequently.

- To serve, cut the pork into diagonal slices 1/2 inch thick. Divide the pork among 8 serving plates. Drizzle with the sauce.

Serves 8

Pork Medallions with Currants and Scotch

Delicious served with potatoes or pasta.

1/3 cup currants
1/2 cup Scotch whisky
2 pork tenderloins (about 1 pound each)
Salt and pepper to taste
2 tablespoons butter
3 tablespoons Dijon mustard
3 tablespoons brown sugar
1/2 cup chicken broth
1 teaspoon thyme

- Combine the currants and Scotch in a small bowl and mix well.

- Cut the pork into 3/4-inch medallions. Season with salt and pepper.

- Heat the butter in a heavy skillet over medium-high heat. Add the medallions. Cook for 1 minute on each side or until brown. Remove to a platter and keep warm.

- Drain the currants, reserving the liquid. Add the reserved liquid to the skillet. Add the Dijon mustard, brown sugar, chicken broth and thyme and whisk until smooth.

- Bring to a boil. Cook until thickened, stirring constantly. Reduce the heat. Add the currants and medallions. Cook, covered, for 2 to 3 minutes or until heated through. Serve immediately.

Serves 6 to 8

Life is too short to stuff a cherry tomato.

Pork Tenderloin with Mustard Sauce

A favorite of our family, as well as many guests at Peacock Hill.

Pork:
2 tablespoons vegetable oil
2 tablespoons coarse-grain mustard
1/2 teaspoon salt
1/2 teaspoon black pepper
1 1/2 pounds pork tenderloin
1/4 cup dry white wine or chicken
     broth

Mustard Sauce:
1 3/4 cups whipping cream
1/4 cup coarse-grain mustard
1/4 teaspoon salt
1/8 teaspoon white pepper

- For the pork, mix the oil, 2 tablespoons mustard, 1/2 teaspoon salt and black pepper in a bowl and mix well. Rub over the pork. Place in a large sealable plastic bag. Marinate in the refrigerator for 8 hours.

- Preheat the oven to 450 degrees.

- Place the pork on a greased rack in a shallow baking pan. Bake for 15 minutes.

- Reduce the oven temperature to 400 degrees. Bake for 15 minutes or until a meat thermometer inserted into the thickest portion registers 160 degrees, basting with the wine every 10 minutes.

- For the mustard sauce, combine the cream, 1/4 cup mustard, 1/4 teaspoon salt and white pepper in a small saucepan and mix well. Bring to a boil and reduce the heat. Simmer for 10 minutes or until thickened, stirring constantly.

- To serve, cut the pork into slices and serve with the mustard sauce.

Serves 4 or 5

Pork Tenderloin with Caramelized Pears

Caramelized Pears:
2 tablespoons butter
4 firm large pears such as Bosc
    pears, cut into 1/3-inch wedges
1 teaspoon sugar

Pork:
1 1/4 pounds pork tenderloin,
    cut into 1-inch slices
1 tablespoon butter
Salt and pepper to taste
1 tablespoon butter
1/3 cup chopped shallots
1/4 teaspoon thyme
1/4 cup brandy
1 cup heavy cream
1/3 cup pear nectar

Pear nectar usually comes in a large container. You can pour the desired amount of juice into paper cups and place in the freezer. When frozen, remove from the cups to sealable plastic freezer bags. Store in the freezer until ready to use.

- For the caramelized pears, melt 2 tablespoons butter in a skillet. Add the pears and sugar. Sauté for 8 minutes or until the pears are tender and deep golden brown.

- For the pork, place the pork between 2 pieces of waxed paper. Pound until 1/4 inch thick.

- Melt 1 tablespoon butter in a large skillet over high heat. Season the pork with salt and pepper. Sauté the pork in batches in the melted butter for 2 minutes on each side or until cooked through, removing each batch to a warm platter. Cover and keep warm.

- Reduce the heat to medium. Melt 1 tablespoon butter in the skillet. Add the shallots and thyme. Sauté for 2 minutes. Add the brandy. Boil for 2 minutes or until the liquid is reduced to a glaze consistency, stirring to deglaze the skillet. Add the cream and nectar. Boil for 5 minutes or until thickened, stirring constantly. Season with salt and pepper.

- To serve, spoon the caramelized pears into the center of a serving platter. Arrange the pork around the pears. Pour the sauce over the pork.

Serves 4

Pork Tenderloin in Lime Sauce

A real treat for two people or more. We enjoy this entrée in the summer months.

Pork:
2 tablespoons vegetable oil
1 1/4 pounds pork tenderloin

Lime Sauce:
2 tablespoons butter
2 tablespoons chopped onion
2 tablespoons chopped shallots
1/4 cup white wine
1 (10-ounce) can chicken broth
1/2 cup beef broth
1 cup heavy cream
2 tablespoons lime juice
Pepper to taste

- Preheat the oven to 400 degrees.

- For the pork, heat the oil in a large heavy ovenproof skillet over high heat. Add the pork. Cook until brown on all sides, turning frequently. Bake for 20 minutes or until a meat thermometer inserted in the thickest portion registers 160 degrees.

- For the lime sauce, melt the butter in a large skillet over medium heat. Add the onion and shallots. Sauté for 3 minutes. Add the wine. Boil for 5 minutes or until the liquid is reduced by 1/2, stirring occasionally. Add the chicken broth and beef broth. Boil for 13 minutes or until the liquid is reduced to 6 tablespoons, stirring frequently. Add the cream. Boil for 7 minutes or until the sauce is reduced to 1 cup, stirring frequently. Stir in the lime juice. Season with pepper.

- To serve, cut the pork diagonally into 1/4-inch slices. Spoon the sauce onto serving plates. Fan the pork atop the sauce.

Serves 2 or 3

Roast Pork

Smells so good while cooking and tastes even better.

1 (4-pound) pork loin
2 tablespoons vegetable oil
4 teaspoons cider vinegar
3 garlic cloves
2 tablespoons fresh oregano, or
  1 tablespoon dried oregano
2 teaspoons salt
1 teaspoon ground pepper

- Arrange the pork in a foil-lined roasting pan. Cut holes all over the sides and top of the pork with a sharp paring knife.

- Process the oil, cider vinegar, garlic, oregano, salt and pepper in a blender until smooth. Spread over the pork, rubbing into the holes made by the knife. Let stand for 15 to 20 minutes.

- Preheat the oven to 400 degrees.

- Bake the roast for 10 minutes. Reduce the oven temperature to 350 degrees. Bake for 1 1/4 hours longer or until a meat thermometer inserted into the thickest portion registers 160 degrees. Remove from the oven. Let stand for 15 minutes before slicing.

Serves 10

Pork Chops in Sour Cream Sauce

Comfort food at its best. Even a good company dish.

4 large pork chops
Sage to taste
Salt and pepper to taste
1 tablespoon vegetable oil
$1/2$ onion, sliced
$1/2$ cup light sour cream
1 teaspoon Dijon mustard
1 tablespoon flour
$1/2$ cup chicken broth
$1/4$ cup dry white wine
$1/4$ cup chopped fresh parsley

- Preheat the oven to 350 degrees.

- Sprinkle the pork with sage, salt and pepper. Heat the oil in a large skillet over medium heat. Add the pork. Cook for 5 minutes on each side or until brown.

- Arrange the pork in a baking dish sprayed with nonstick cooking spray, reserving the drippings in the skillet. Layer the onion over the pork. Mix the sour cream, Dijon mustard and flour in a small bowl until blended.

- Pour the chicken broth and wine in the reserved drippings in the skillet. Boil for 1 minute. Add the sour cream mixture and parsley and whisk to blend well. Pour over the pork and onion.

- Bake, uncovered, for 20 to 25 minutes or until cooked through and bubbly.

Serves 4

The purpose of life is a life of purpose.

Baked Country Ham

Hard-to-beat good country ham.

1 (12- to 14-pound) country ham
2 teaspoons whole cloves
8 cups apple juice or cider
1/2 cup packed brown sugar
2 teaspoons ground cloves
Dry sherry

- Place the ham in a large container and cover with cold water. Soak for 16 hours in the refrigerator, draining and replacing the water once.

- Drain the ham. Scrub in warm water with a stiff brush and rinse well. Remove the skin from the ham and trim off the fat. Insert the whole cloves in the ham.

- Preheat the oven to 325 degrees.

- Place the ham fat side up in a large roasting pan. Insert a meat thermometer into the thickest portion. Pour the apple juice over the ham. Bake, covered, for 4 to 4 1/2 hours or until the meat thermometer registers 160 degrees. Drain the pan juices.

- Mix the brown sugar and ground cloves in a small bowl. Add just enough sherry to form a paste. Spread over the fat side of the ham. Bake the ham, uncovered, for 30 minutes or until the meat thermometer registers 170 degrees. Let stand for 15 to 20 minutes before slicing.

- Arrange the ham on a large serving platter. Garnish with Seckel pears and lemon leaves.

Serves 25 to 30

Heavenly Sole

1 pound sole fillets
1 tablespoon fresh lemon juice
1/4 cup freshly grated Parmesan
  cheese
2 tablespoons butter, softened
1 1/2 tablespoons mayonnaise
1 1/2 tablespoons chopped green
  onions
Salt to taste

- Preheat the broiler. Arrange the fish in a single layer on a well-greased bake-and-serve platter. Brush with the lemon juice. Let stand for 8 to 10 minutes.

- Combine the Parmesan cheese, butter, mayonnaise, green onions and salt in a small bowl and stir to blend well. Broil the fish 4 inches from the heat source for 5 to 7 minutes or until the fish flakes easily. Remove from the heat. Spread the Parmesan cheese mixture over the fish.

- Broil for 1 to 2 minutes longer or until light brown.

Serves 3

Side Dishes

It is better to eat

vegetables with those

who love you than

to eat meat with those

who hate you.

Proverbs 15:17
New Century Version

Fresh Asparagus with Hollandaise Sauce

1 pound fresh asparagus, trimmed
1/2 cup (1 stick) butter, softened
4 egg yolks
3 tablespoons lemon juice
7 tablespoons (about) hot water
Salt and white pepper to taste

- Steam the asparagus in a steamer until tender-crisp.

- Cream the butter in a mixing bowl until light and fluffy. Add the egg yolks 1 at a time, beating well after each addition. Add the lemon juice and water and mix well.

- Pour into a double boiler. Cook for a few minutes or until thickened, stirring constantly. Season with salt and white pepper.

- Serve the sauce over the asparagus.

Serves 4 to 6

Angel Asparagus

1/4 cup olive oil
Grated zest of 1 lemon
2 garlic cloves, minced
White part only of 4 leeks,
  chopped
Salt and pepper to taste
1 pound fresh asparagus
1 tablespoon chopped fresh chives
2 tablespoons white wine
2 tablespoons unsalted butter
16 ounces uncooked angel hair
  pasta
1/2 tablespoon chopped fresh
  chives
Freshly grated Parmesan cheese

- Combine the olive oil, lemon zest, garlic, leeks, salt and pepper in a sauté pan. Simmer, partially covered, over medium heat for 4 to 6 minutes or until the leeks are tender, stirring occasionally.

- Cut 1/2 of the asparagus into 1 1/2-inch lengths. Add the asparagus pieces, 1 tablespoon chives, wine, butter, salt and pepper to the leek mixture. Cook for 2 to 3 minutes or until the asparagus is heated through.

- Fill an asparagus pan with salted water. Bring to a boil. Add the remaining asparagus tips side up. Cook, covered, for 2 to 3 minutes or until tender, but still firm to the bite.

- Cook the pasta using the package directions. Drain the pasta, reserving 1/2 cup liquid. Return the pasta to the saucepan. Add the asparagus and leek sauce and the reserved liquid and toss to coat well.

- To serve, arrange the pasta mixture on serving plates or in pasta bowls. Top with the asparagus, tips 1/2 tablespoon chives and Parmesan cheese.

Serves 6 to 8 as a side dish, or 4 or 5 as a main dish

Asparagus and New Potatoes

12 ounces asparagus, trimmed
8 unpeeled tiny new potatoes, cut
    into quarters
2 teaspoons olive oil
1/2 teaspoon grated lemon zest
1/4 teaspoon salt
1/4 teaspoon thyme

- Cut the asparagus into 2-inch pieces.

- Cook the potatoes in water to cover in a saucepan for 10 minutes. Add the asparagus. Cook for 8 minutes; drain.

- Mix the olive oil, lemon zest, salt and thyme in a small bowl. Add to the vegetables and toss to coat. Serve warm.

Serves 4 to 6

Asparagus with Orange Dressing and Toasted Hazelnuts

2 tablespoons finely chopped
    hazelnuts
1 1/2 pounds asparagus
Salt to taste
2 teaspoons fresh orange juice
1 teaspoon fresh lemon juice
1 tablespoon olive oil
1/4 teaspoon freshly grated orange
    zest
Pepper to taste

- Preheat the oven to 375 degrees.

- Bake the hazelnuts in a small shallow baking pan for 4 to 5 minutes or until toasted and golden brown.

- Trim the asparagus ends. Peel the lower 2 inches of the stems with a vegetable peeler if desired. Cook in boiling salted water in a large saucepan for 6 minutes or until tender-crisp; drain well in a colander.

- Combine the orange juice, lemon juice, olive oil, orange zest, salt and pepper in a small bowl and whisk to blend well.

- Arrange the asparagus on individual serving plates. Spoon the orange dressing over the top and sprinkle with the toasted hazelnuts.

Serves 4

Broccoli and Brie with Pasta

Salt to taste
5 quarts water
8 ounces uncooked spaghetti
1 1/2 tablespoons olive oil
1 bunch broccoli, cut into florets
1 garlic clove, minced
8 ounces Brie cheese, rind
    removed, cut into 1-inch pieces
1/2 cup walnuts, toasted, coarsely
    chopped
Pepper to taste

- Bring the salted water to a boil in a large stockpot. Add the pasta. Cook until al dente. Drain the pasta, reserving 1/3 cup of the cooking liquid. Return the pasta and the reserved liquid to the stockpot.

- Heat the olive oil in a large heavy skillet over medium heat until hot but not smoking. Add the broccoli and salt to taste. Cook for 5 minutes or until tender-crisp. Add the garlic. Cook for 30 seconds.

- Add the broccoli mixture, Brie cheese and walnuts to the hot pasta and toss until the Brie cheese is melted. Season with salt and pepper.

Serves 4 to 6 as a side dish, or 2 as a main dish

Carrot Bundles

2 pounds carrots, trimmed
10 green onions
2/3 cup fresh lemon juice
6 tablespoons butter
1/4 cup sugar
1/2 teaspoon salt

- Cut the carrots into 3-inch sticks. Steam in a steamer until tender-crisp. Rinse in cold water and remove to paper towels to drain. Separate into 10 bundles.

- Remove the white bulbs from the green onions and reserve for another use. Dip the green stems into boiling water for 30 seconds. Tie into a double knot around each carrot bundle while still limp and trim the ends.

- Combine the lemon juice, butter, sugar and salt in a large saucepan. Bring to a boil and reduce the heat. Simmer until the sugar and salt are dissolved.

- Add the carrot bundles carefully. Cook until just heated through, spooning the lemon mixture over the bundles frequently. Remove each bundle carefully from the saucepan with a spatula. Serve hot.

Serves 10

Julienned Carrots

2 tablespoons butter or olive oil
2 pounds carrots, julienned
1/4 cup sweet vermouth
Salt and freshly ground pepper to
    taste
2 tablespoons chopped fresh parsley

- Heat the butter in a skillet until melted. Add the carrots. Sauté until the carrots just begin to turn brown. Stir in the vermouth.

- Simmer for 5 minutes, stirring frequently. Season with salt and pepper.

- Spoon into a serving bowl. Sprinkle with the parsley.

Serves 6 to 8

Green Beans with Balsamic Shallot Butter

Delicious, but different.

1/2 cup balsamic vinegar
2 large shallots, finely chopped
1/4 cup (1/2 stick) butter, softened
2 pounds green beans, trimmed
Salt and pepper to taste

- Combine the vinegar and shallots in a small heavy saucepan and mix well. Bring to a boil over medium heat. Cook for 6 minutes or until the liquid is reduced to 1 tablespoon, stirring frequently. Spoon into a small bowl and cool completely. Add the butter and mix with a fork to blend.

- Cook the green beans in a large pan of boiling water for 6 minutes or until tender-crisp; drain. Plunge immediately into cold water; drain. Pat dry with paper towels.

- The balsamic butter and green beans can be prepared 1 day ahead and stored, covered, separately in the refrigerator.

- Combine the green beans and balsamic butter in a large skillet. Sauté over medium heat for 5 minutes or until heated through. Season with salt and pepper to taste.

Serves 8

Green Beans and Carrots

2 pounds slender green beans,
    trimmed
Salt to taste
8 ounces carrots, peeled, julienned
2 tablespoons butter
2 tablespoons olive oil
Paul Prudhomme's vegetable
    seasoning or salt and pepper
    to taste

- Cook the green beans in boiling salted water in a large saucepan for 6 minutes or until tender-crisp. Remove the green beans with a slotted spoon to a large bowl filled with ice water.

- Add the carrots to the boiling water. Cook for 1 minute or until tender-crisp. Remove the carrots with a slotted spoon to the ice water with the green beans.

- Drain the green beans and carrots and pat dry.

- The vegetables may be prepared a day ahead, wrapped in paper towels and refrigerated until ready to use.

- Melt the butter with the olive oil in a large saucepan over medium-high heat. Add the vegetables. Sauté for 2 minutes or until the vegetables are heated through. Season with vegetable seasoning.

Serves 12

Sesame Green Beans

2 medium carrots, julienned
1 tablespoon butter
2 pounds young and tender green
    beans, trimmed
3 tablespoons soy sauce
1 tablespoon vegetable oil
1 tablespoon sesame oil
2 teaspoons sesame seeds, toasted

- Sauté the carrots in the butter in a small skillet for 2 to 3 minutes or until tender-crisp. Remove to a bowl.

- Cook the green beans in boiling water in a saucepan for 10 minutes; drain. Add the soy sauce and vegetable oil. Cook over medium heat for 10 minutes, stirring frequently.

- Add the carrots to the green beans. Stir in the sesame oil. Sprinkle with the sesame seeds.

Serves 4 or 5

Black-Eyed Peas and Rice

A Creole dish–delicious and spicy.

1 (16-ounce) package dried
   black-eyed peas
1 ham hock
3 cups chopped onions
1 bunch green onions, chopped
1 cup chopped fresh parsley
1 cup chopped green bell pepper
2 garlic cloves, minced
1 teaspoon salt
1 teaspoon red pepper
1 teaspoon black pepper
3 dashes of hot sauce, or to taste
1 tablespoon Worcestershire sauce
1 (8-ounce) can tomato sauce
1/4 teaspoon oregano
1/4 teaspoon thyme
Hot cooked rice

- Sort the peas and rinse well. Place in a Dutch oven and cover with water. Soak for 8 to 12 hours.

- Drain the peas. Add the ham hock and cover with water. Cook, covered, over low heat for 45 minutes.

- Add the onions, green onions, parsley, bell pepper, garlic, salt, red pepper, black pepper, hot sauce, Worcestershire sauce, tomato sauce, oregano and thyme.

- Bring to a boil and reduce the heat. Simmer, uncovered, for 45 to 60 minutes, stirring occasionally.

- To serve, ladle over the hot rice in a serving bowl. Garnish with a green onion fan.

Serves 10

After soaking the black-eyed peas, you can cook with the ham hock in a slow cooker on Low for 6 to 8 hours. The black-eyed peas will keep their shape by cooking in a slow cooker.

Hopping John

1 onion, chopped
1/4 cup chopped green bell pepper
2 teaspoons vegetable oil
1 (14-ounce) can tomatoes,
    drained, chopped
2 or 3 garlic cloves, minced
4 cups frozen black-eyed peas
1 cup uncooked rice
2 cups chicken broth
1 ham hock
Salt and black pepper to taste
Pinch of cayenne pepper
3/4 cup chopped green onions
1/2 cup chopped Italian parsley

- Sauté the onion and bell pepper in the oil in a saucepan over medium heat for 5 minutes or until the onion is translucent. Add the tomatoes, garlic and peas.

- Cook for 5 minutes.

- Add the rice, chicken broth, ham hock, salt, black pepper and cayenne pepper.

- Bring to a boil and reduce the heat. Simmer for 45 to 60 minutes or until the rice is tender and the liquid is absorbed.

- Sprinkle with the green onions and parsley.

Serves 4 to 6

Gruyère Potato Casserole

1 pound large red potatoes
Salt to taste
3/4 cup coarsely grated Gruyère
    cheese
Pepper to taste
1 egg
1 cup milk, scalded

- Preheat the oven to 400 degrees.

- Peel the potatoes. Cut into thin slices about 1/8 inch thick. Add the potatoes to boiling salted water in a large saucepan.

- Parboil for 4 minutes. Drain well in a colander.

- Arrange 1/3 of the potatoes in a buttered 1 1/2-quart gratin or shallow baking dish. Sprinkle with 1/4 cup of the cheese and salt and pepper to taste. Layer 1/2 of the remaining potatoes over the cheese. Sprinkle with 1/2 of the remaining cheese and salt and pepper to taste. Layer the remaining potatoes over the top.

- Whisk the egg in a small bowl. Add the hot milk in a fine stream, beating constantly with a whisk. Season with salt and pepper to taste. Pour evenly over the layers. Sprinkle with the remaining cheese.

- Bake for 30 minutes or until the potatoes are tender and the top is golden brown.

Serves 2 to 4

Southwestern Spuds

1 1/2 pounds baking potatoes,
    peeled, cut into quarters
3 tablespoons butter
1 1/2 cups whole kernel corn
1 teaspoon chili powder
1/2 cup thinly sliced scallions
1/2 to 3/4 cup hot milk
1/2 teaspoon salt
1/4 teaspoon pepper
1 cup (4 ounces) shredded sharp
    Cheddar cheese
2 ounces Pepper Jack cheese,
    finely chopped

- Place the potatoes in a large saucepan. Add enough water to cover by 1 inch. Bring to a boil and reduce the heat to medium. Cook, covered, for 15 to 20 minutes or until the potatoes are tender.

- Melt the butter in a large skillet. Add the corn. Cook for 2 minutes, stirring constantly. Add the chili powder and scallions. Cook for 1 to 2 minutes or until the scallions are tender. Remove from the heat.

- Drain the potatoes in a colander. Return the hot potatoes to the saucepan. Mash the potatoes until fairly smooth. Add 1/2 cup hot milk gradually, mashing until the potatoes are fluffy and adding the remaining milk if needed. Season with the salt and pepper.

- Return the saucepan to low heat. Cook until the potatoes are hot, stirring constantly. Add the Cheddar cheese, Pepper Jack cheese and corn mixture and stir to mix well.

Serves 6 to 8

Special Spuds

Special—special.

6 cups mashed cooked potatoes
8 ounces whipped cream cheese
    with chives
2 eggs
1/4 cup sour cream
1/4 cup (1/2 stick) unsalted butter,
    softened
Pinch of salt

- Preheat the oven to 400 degrees.

- Combine the mashed potatoes, cream cheese, eggs, sour cream, butter and salt in a large mixing bowl and beat until smooth.

- Pour into a greased soufflé dish.

- Bake for 45 minutes or until light brown.

Serves 6 to 8

Mashed Potatoes and Ham

6 medium potatoes (4 pounds)
3/4 cup hot milk
1/2 cup sour cream
1/4 cup (1/2 stick) butter, softened
1/2 teaspoon salt
1/8 teaspoon ground red pepper
1 garlic clove, minced
1/4 cup shredded Gruyère cheese
2 green onions, thinly sliced
1/3 cup chopped baked ham
   (optional)

- Peel the potatoes and cut into 1-inch cubes. Cook in boiling water to cover in a saucepan for 15 minutes or until tender; drain.

- Mash the potatoes. Add the milk, sour cream, butter, salt, red pepper and garlic and mix well. Stir in the cheese, green onions and ham.

- Spoon into a serving dish. Garnish with additional sliced green onions.

Serves 6 to 8

Fanned Baked Potatoes

4 medium baking potatoes
1 1/2 teaspoons salt
Pepper to taste
3 or 4 tablespoons melted butter
3 to 4 tablespoons chopped fresh
   chives or parsley
2 teaspoons herbs of choice, such
   as rosemary, thyme, sage, etc.
1/4 cup shredded Cheddar cheese
2 tablespoons grated Parmesan
   cheese

- Preheat the oven to 425 degrees.

- Scrub the potatoes well. Cut into thin slices, but not all of the way through.

- Arrange the potatoes in a baking dish, fanning each apart slightly. Sprinkle with the salt and pepper. Drizzle with the butter. Sprinkle with the herbs.

- Bake for 45 to 50 minutes or until tender. Remove from the oven. Sprinkle with Cheddar cheese and Parmesan cheese.

- Bake for 10 to 15 minutes or until light brown. Serve immediately.

Serves 4

Overnight Mashed Potatoes

8 to 10 medium potatoes
8 ounces cream cheese, softened
1 cup sour cream
1/2 cup (1 stick) butter, melted
1/4 cup chopped chives
1/8 teaspoon garlic powder
2 teaspoons salt
Paprika to taste

- Scrub the potatoes well. Cook in boiling water to cover in a saucepan for 30 minutes or until tender; drain. Mash the potatoes until smooth.

- Beat the cream cheese at medium speed in a mixing bowl until smooth. Add the potatoes, sour cream, butter, chives, garlic powder and salt and beat until blended.

- Spoon into a buttered 2-quart baking dish. Sprinkle with paprika. Chill, covered, for 8 to 12 hours.

- Preheat the oven to 350 degrees.

- Remove the potato mixture from the refrigerator. Let stand at room temperature for 15 minutes.

- Bake, uncovered, for 30 minutes or until bubbly.

Serves 6 to 8

Super Whipped Potatoes

These potatoes are so good, you may not want anything else to eat.

7 to 8 baking potatoes (about
    2 1/2 pounds)
2 carrots, sliced
4 to 6 garlic cloves, peeled
1/4 teaspoon salt
1/2 to 3/4 cup buttermilk
1 to 2 tablespoons butter
1/2 teaspoon salt
Pepper to taste
3 tablespoons chopped fresh parsley

- Peel the potatoes and cut into halves lengthwise. Place the potatoes, carrots and garlic in a large saucepan. Cover with water. Add 1/4 teaspoon salt. Bring to a boil over high heat. Reduce the heat to low. Cook, covered, for 20 minutes or until the vegetables are tender; drain thoroughly.

- Add the buttermilk gradually, beating with an electric mixer until light and fluffy and adding additional buttermilk if needed. Beat in the butter gradually. Add 1/2 teaspoon salt, pepper and parsley and stir to mix well.

- Serve immediately or place over hot water if not ready to serve.

Serves 6

Mini Baked Red Potatoes

Very tasty.

20 small red potatoes
1 cup sour cream
1/2 cup crumbled bacon

- Preheat the oven to 350 degrees.

- Scrub the potatoes. Arrange on a baking sheet.

- Bake for 30 minutes.

- Cut the potatoes into halves. Scoop out the centers with a spoon or melon baller and place in a bowl, reserving the potato shells.

- Add the sour cream and bacon to the potato pulp and mix well. Pipe or spoon into the reserved potato shells.

- Note: You may sprinkle the bacon on top instead of mixing in with the potatoes.

Serves 8 to 10

Basil New Potatoes

10 small new red potatoes, cut
   into quarters
1/4 cup (1/2 stick) butter
2 tablespoons vegetable oil
1/2 onion, chopped
1/4 cup chopped fresh basil, or
   1 tablespoon dried basil
3 tablespoons chopped fresh parsley
1 1/2 teaspoons salt
1 teaspoon oregano
1/4 cup chopped roasted red bell
   pepper
Pepper to taste

- Cook the potatoes in boiling water to cover in a saucepan for 15 minutes or until tender; drain.

- Melt the butter and oil in a saucepan. Add the potatoes, onion, basil, parsley, salt, oregano, roasted bell pepper and pepper and toss to mix well.

Serves 4

Roasted New Potatoes

These potatoes are easy to prepare and bake. Serve with most any entrée.

2 to 3 tablespoons canola oil
2 garlic cloves, minced
1 teaspoon salt
Pepper to taste
1/2 teaspoon rosemary
6 unpeeled red new potatoes,
    cut into quarters

- Preheat the oven to 400 degrees.

- Mix the canola oil, garlic, salt, pepper and rosemary in a large bowl. Add the potatoes and toss to coat. Arrange the potatoes on a baking sheet.

- Bake for 50 to 55 minutes or until crisp and golden brown, stirring occasionally.

Serves 2 or 3

Herbed New Potatoes

2 pounds small red potatoes
3 to 4 tablespoons olive oil
1 garlic clove, minced
1 teaspoon salt
1 tablespoon chopped fresh
    rosemary
1 tablespoon chopped fresh thyme,
    or 1 teaspoon dried thyme

- Combine the potatoes and olive oil in a saucepan and toss to coat. Cook over medium heat, for 25 to 35 minutes or until brown, stirring occasionally.

- Add the garlic, salt, rosemary and thyme and toss to mix well. Cook, covered, until the potatoes are tender.

Serves 4 to 6

Last night, I dreamed I ate a five-pound marshmallow;
when I woke up, my pillow was gone.

Bourbon Sweet Potatoes

10 medium sweet potatoes
3/4 cup (1 1/2 sticks) butter
1/3 cup bourbon
1/2 teaspoon salt
1/2 cup coarsely chopped walnuts
2 tablespoons butter

- Preheat the oven to 400 degrees.

- Scrub the sweet potatoes well. Trim the sweet potatoes and pierce with a fork several times. Arrange on a baking sheet.

- Bake for 1 hour or until tender. Remove from the oven and cool until easily handled. Peel the sweet potatoes, discarding the skins.

- Reduce the oven temperature to 350 degrees.

- Combine the sweet potato pulp, 3/4 cup butter, bourbon and salt in a mixing bowl. Beat at medium speed until light and fluffy.

- Reserve 2 tablespoons of the walnuts for the topping. Stir the remaining walnuts into the sweet potato mixture. Spoon into a lightly greased 1 1/2-quart baking dish. Dot with 2 tablespoons butter. Sprinkle with the reserved walnuts.

- Bake for 20 minutes.

Serves 8

Glazed Sweet Potatoes

8 cups sweet potatoes, peeled, cut
　　into cubes (about 3 pounds)
1/4 cup lemon sections (about
　　1 large lemon)
4 cups water
1/4 cup packed dark brown sugar
2 tablespoons butter
1/8 teaspoon red pepper
3 tablespoon maple syrup
1/2 teaspoon cinnamon
Dash of salt

- Place the sweet potatoes, lemon sections and water in a large saucepan. Bring to a boil. Cook for 20 minutes or until tender, stirring occasionally.

- Remove the sweet potatoes with a slotted spoon to a bowl, reserving the cooking liquid in the saucepan.

- Bring the reserved cooking liquid to a boil. Cook for 12 minutes or until the mixture is reduced to 1/3 cup. Add the brown sugar, butter, red pepper, maple syrup, cinnamon and salt and stir to mix well. Stir in the sweet potatoes.

- Cook for 2 minutes or until heated through.

Serves 12

Sweet Potatoes with Brandy Sauce

Brandy Sauce:

1 tablespoon cornstarch
1 tablespoon water
2/3 cup packed brown sugar
3/4 cup water
2 tablespoons butter
1/4 cup raisins
1/2 teaspoon nutmeg
2 tablespoons lemon juice
1/4 cup brandy
1/2 to 1 cup sliced unpeeled green
    apples

Sweet Potatoes:

4 large sweet potatoes
6 tablespoons butter

- For the brandy sauce, dissolve the cornstarch in 1 tablespoon water in a medium saucepan. Add the brown sugar and 3/4 cup water and mix well. Add 2 tablespoons butter and raisins and mix well.

- Bring to a boil, stirring constantly. Cook until thick and glossy, stirring constantly.

- Remove from the heat and let stand until partially cooled. Add the nutmeg, lemon juice and brandy and mix well. Stir in the apples.

- Preheat the oven to 350 degrees.

- For the sweet potatoes, scrub the sweet potatoes. Cook in boiling water to cover in a large saucepan until tender; drain and cool.

- Peel the sweet potatoes, discarding the skins. Cut into slices 1/4 inch thick.

- Layer the sweet potatoes in a generously buttered large shallow baking dish, dotting with 6 tablespoons butter.

- Reserve a small amount of the brandy sauce for basting. Spoon the remaining brandy sauce over the sweet potatoes, fitting the raisins and apples from the sauce between the sweet potatoes.

- Bake for 30 minutes, basting occasionally with the reserved brandy sauce.

Serves 16 to 20

Roasted Sweet Potatoes

Very tasty.

2¼ pounds sweet potatoes, peeled,
cut into 1½-inch pieces (about
7 cups)
6 tablespoons butter
3 tablespoons honey
1 teaspoon fresh lemon juice
Salt and pepper to taste

- Preheat the oven to 350 degrees.

- Arrange the sweet potatoes in a 9×13-inch baking dish.

- Mix the butter, honey and lemon juice in a small saucepan. Cook over medium heat until the butter melts, stirring frequently. Pour over the sweet potatoes and toss to coat. Sprinkle with salt and pepper.

- Bake for 50 minutes or until tender when pierced with a fork, stirring and turning occasionally.

Serves 4

Sautéed Sweet Potatoes

2 pounds sweet potatoes
2 teaspoons butter
Brown sugar to taste (optional)

- Scrub the sweet potatoes. Peel the sweet potatoes and cut into slices ½ inch thick.

- Melt the butter in a 12-inch skillet over medium heat. Stir in the brown sugar. Add the sweet potatoes.

- Cook, covered, for 20 minutes or until the potatoes are tender and golden, turning once.

Serves 6

Spinach Soufflé

1/4 cup (1/2 stick) butter
1/4 cup flour
1/2 teaspoon salt
Dash of pepper
1 cup (4 ounces) shredded sharp
  Cheddar cheese
3/4 cup milk
1 (10-ounce) package frozen
  chopped spinach, cooked,
  drained
2 tablespoons chopped onion
4 eggs, separated

- Preheat the oven to 350 degrees.

- Heat the butter and flour in a large saucepan over low heat until smooth and bubbly, stirring constantly. Season with the salt and pepper. Add the Cheddar cheese and milk. Cook over medium heat until the cheese is melted, stirring constantly. Remove from the heat.

- Add the spinach and onion and mix well. Add the egg yolks gradually, mixing well after each addition. Let stand until cool.

- Beat the egg whites in a mixing bowl until stiff peaks form. Fold into the spinach mixture. Pour into a lightly greased 2-quart soufflé dish or individual soufflé dishes.

- Bake for 35 minutes or until set.

Serves 10

Spinach Soufflé with Creamed Vegetable Sauce

Spinach Soufflé:
2 (10-ounce) packages frozen
  chopped spinach
1/2 cup bread crumbs
1/2 teaspoon salt
1/8 teaspoon pepper
1/2 cup milk
2 eggs, beaten
3/4 cup slivered almonds
5 tablespoons butter, melted

Creamed Vegetable Sauce:
1/4 cup (1/2 stick) butter
1/3 cup chopped onions
1/4 cup flour
2 cups milk
1/2 cup chopped cooked carrots
1/2 cup cooked green peas
1/2 cup cooked chopped celery

- Preheat the oven to 325 degrees.

- For the soufflé, cook the spinach in a saucepan using the package directions; drain well.

- Combine the spinach, bread crumbs, salt, pepper, 1/2 cup milk, eggs, almonds and 5 tablespoons butter in a bowl and mix well. Spoon into a greased 1-quart round baking dish.

- Bake for 45 to 60 minutes or until set. Remove from the oven to cool slightly before serving.

- For the sauce, melt 1/4 cup butter in a saucepan. Add the onions. Cook until tender but not brown. Stir in the flour. Add the milk gradually, stirring constantly. Cook until thickened and smooth, stirring constantly. Add the carrots, peas and celery. Cook until heated through.

- To serve, pour the sauce over the soufflé.

Serves 6 to 8

Acorn Squash

2 medium acorn squash
4 teaspoons butter
4 teaspoons honey
4 pinches of ginger
4 pinches of cinnamon
Salt to taste

- Preheat the oven to 325 degrees.

- Rinse the squash and pat dry. Remove a slice 1/4 inch thick from the blossom end of each squash. Stand the squash on this level base. Cut into halves from the stem to the blossom end. Cut a slice 1/8 inch thick from the bottom of each squash half so the squash will sit evenly in a baking pan. Scoop out the seeds and stringy insides with a spoon.

- Arrange the squash halves in a baking pan. Place 1 teaspoon butter, 1 teaspoon honey, pinch of ginger, pinch of cinnamon and salt in each squash cavity.

- Bake on the middle oven rack for 40 to 50 minutes or until the squash halves are soft and mushy.

- Serve while very hot.

Serves 4

Roasted Summer Squash

2 cups thinly sliced yellow squash
1/2 teaspoon vegetable oil
1/4 teaspoon paprika
1/8 teaspoon salt
1/8 teaspoon garlic powder

- Preheat the oven to 450 degrees.

- Place the squash, oil, paprika, salt and garlic powder in a large sealable plastic bag. Seal the bag and shake to coat the squash.

- Arrange the squash in a single layer on a baking sheet sprayed with nonstick cooking spray.

- Bake for 20 minutes, turning after 10 minutes.

Makes 2 cups

Stuffed Yellow Squash

3 medium yellow squash
1/4 cup chopped onion
3 garlic cloves, minced
2 teaspoons olive oil
3 plum tomatoes, peeled, seeded,
    chopped
2 tablespoons chopped fresh
    oregano
1/4 teaspoon salt
1/4 teaspoon pepper
1/3 cup fine dry bread crumbs
1 1/2 tablespoons shredded
    Parmesan cheese

- Preheat the oven to 375 degrees.

- Cook the squash in boiling water to cover in a saucepan until tender; drain. Plunge immediately into ice water to stop the cooking process; drain.

- Cut the squash into halves lengthwise. Scoop out the seeds and discard.

- Sauté the onion and garlic in the olive oil in a saucepan for 5 minutes or until tender. Stir in the tomatoes, oregano, salt and pepper. Cook until heated through. Stir in the bread crumbs.

- Spoon the tomato mixture into the squash halves. Sprinkle with the Parmesan cheese. Arrange on a baking sheet.

- Bake, covered, for 25 minutes or until heated through.

Serves 6

Tomato Broccoli Cups

This colorful side dish can be prepared ahead and baked later.

1 tablespoon butter
1 tablespoon vegetable oil
2 cups chopped broccoli
5 or 6 mushrooms, chopped
1 garlic clove, minced
1/4 teaspoon salt
Pepper to taste
3 tomatoes, cut into halves
Freshly grated Parmesan cheese
    to taste

- Preheat the oven to 350 degrees.

- Melt the butter with the oil in a skillet over medium heat. Add the broccoli, mushrooms and garlic. Sauté for 10 minutes or until the vegetables are crisp. Season with the salt and pepper.

- Remove the pulp from the tomatoes, leaving a 1/4-inch shell. Drain cut side down on paper towels for 5 minutes.

- Arrange the tomatoes on a baking sheet. Fill with the vegetable mixture. Sprinkle with Parmesan cheese.

- Bake for 15 minutes or until the tomatoes are heated through.

- Serve immediately.

Serves 6

Zucchini and Carrots

Serve in a red cabbage leaf with a pinch of thyme for a dramatic effect.

12 ounces carrots, cut into
   julienne strips
12 ounces zucchini, cut into
   julienne strips
1/2 cup (1 stick) unsalted butter,
   melted
Salt and pepper to taste

- Steam the carrots over boiling water in a steamer. Layer the zucchini on top of the carrots. Steam until tender-crisp.

- Spoon the vegetables into a heated serving dish. Add the butter and toss to coat. Season with salt and pepper.

Serves 6

Zucchini and Tomatoes

2 medium zucchini (12 ounces)
1/2 cup chopped onion
1 teaspoon basil
2 teaspoons olive oil
2 medium tomatoes, peeled,
   chopped
1/2 teaspoon salt
1/8 to 1/4 teaspoon pepper

- Cut the zucchini into 1/4-inch slices.

- Sauté the onion and basil in the olive oil in a skillet over medium heat for 1 minute. Add the zucchini.

- Cook for 5 minutes, stirring occasionally. Add the tomatoes, salt and pepper.

- Cook for 3 minutes or until tender.

- Serve immediately.

Serves 4 to 6

Lord, grant me patience to endure my blessings.

Stuffed Zucchini

4 medium zucchini
Salt and pepper to taste
2 tablespoons olive oil
3 medium potatoes, cut into cubes
1 tablespoon olive oil
1 medium onion, finely chopped
1 tablespoon olive oil
5 large garlic cloves, minced
3 medium tomatoes, seeded,
   chopped
1/3 cup chopped fresh basil
6 ounces Monterey Jack cheese,
   shredded

- Preheat the oven to 400 degrees.

- Place 2 baking sheets in the oven.

- Cut the zucchini into halves lengthwise. Scoop out the seeds and most of the pulp to within 1/4-inch of the sides. Season with salt and pepper. Brush with 2 tablespoons olive oil. Arrange the zucchini cut side down on 1 of the hot baking sheets. Place on the lowest oven rack.

- Toss the potatoes with 1 tablespoon olive oil, salt and pepper in a bowl. Spread on the remaining hot baking sheet. Place on the upper oven rack.

- Bake the zucchini and potatoes for 10 minutes. Remove the zucchini from the oven. Turn the zucchini over on the baking sheet using tongs.

- Bake the potatoes for 2 minutes longer or until tender.

- Sauté the onion in 1 tablespoon olive oil in a 12-inch skillet until tender. Add the garlic. Cook for 30 seconds.

- Add the tomatoes and cooked potatoes. Cook until heated through, stirring constantly. Remove from the heat. Stir in the basil, 1/2 cup of the cheese, salt and pepper.

- Spoon about 1/2 cup of the potato mixture into each zucchini half, packing lightly. Sprinkle with the remaining cheese. Return to the oven.

- Bake until the zucchini is heated through and the cheese is light brown.

- Serve immediately.

Serves 8 as a side dish, or 4 as a main dish

Simply Zucchini

2 medium zucchini
3 tablespoons butter
Garlic salt to taste
Grated Parmesan cheese to taste

- Rinse the zucchini. Do not peel. Cut into thin slices.

- Melt the butter in a sauté pan. Add the zucchini. Season with garlic salt.

- Cook for 4 minutes or until tender-crisp. Sprinkle with Parmesan cheese.

- Cook until the Parmesan cheese is melted.

- Serve immediately.

Serves 4

Vegetables and Cheese Dish

Best in the summertime when the vegetables are fresh from the garden.

1/2 cup chopped onion
1 garlic clove, minced
3 zucchini, sliced
1 tablespoon vegetable oil
1/2 teaspoon salt
Pepper to taste
1/2 teaspoon dillweed
3 small tomatoes, seeded, peeled,
  sliced, chopped
1 cup (4 ounces) shredded
  Cheddar cheese
1 tablespoon butter
1/2 cup bread crumbs
2 tablespoons grated Parmesan
  cheese

- Preheat the oven to 350 degrees.

- Sauté the onion, garlic and zucchini in the oil in a large skillet for 5 minutes or until tender crisp. Season with salt, pepper and dillweed.

- Layer the zucchini mixture, tomatoes and Cheddar cheese 1/2 at a time in a lightly oiled baking dish.

- Melt the butter in the skillet. Add the bread crumbs and toss to coat. Sprinkle over the layers. Sprinkle Parmesan cheese over the top.

- Bake, uncovered, until bubbly. Serve immediately.

Serves 4 to 6

Macaroni and Cheese

—the "elegant" way.

6 slices French bread, torn into
   1/4-inch pieces
2 tablespoons unsalted butter,
   melted
6 tablespoons unsalted butter
1/2 cup flour
5 1/2 cups milk, heated
2 teaspoons salt
1/4 teaspoon nutmeg
1/4 teaspoon pepper
4 1/2 cups (18 ounces) shredded
   sharp white Cheddar cheese
2 cups (8 ounces) shredded
   Gruyère cheese
16 ounces elbow macaroni

- Preheat the oven to 375 degrees.

- Toss the bread with 2 tablespoons butter in a medium bowl to coat.

- Melt 6 tablespoons butter in a large skillet over medium heat until bubbly. Add the flour. Cook for 1 minute, stirring constantly. Add the hot milk a small amount at a time, stirring constantly. Cook for 8 to 10 minutes or until thickened, stirring constantly. Remove from the heat. Stir in the salt, nutmeg, pepper, 3 cups of the Cheddar cheese and 1 1/2 cups of the Gruyère cheese.

- Fill a large saucepan with salted water and cover. Bring to a boil. Add the macaroni. Cook for 2 to 3 minutes or until partially cooked through. Pour into a colander to drain. Rinse under cold running water; drain.

- Stir the macaroni into the cheese sauce. Pour into a 3-quart baking dish sprayed with nonstick cooking spray. Sprinkle with the remaining Cheddar cheese and Gruyère cheese. Top with the bread.

- Bake for 30 minutes or until golden brown.

Serves 12

Almond Rice

Delicious.

1/3 cup chopped onion
1/3 cup slivered almonds
2 tablespoons butter
1 cup uncooked basmati rice
1/4 cup sherry
1 3/4 cups chicken broth
1/4 teaspoon salt

- Sauté the onion and almonds in the butter in a skillet. Add the rice.

- Sauté until the rice is slightly opaque but not brown.

- Add the sherry, chicken broth and salt.

- Simmer, covered, for 20 to 30 minutes or until the rice is cooked through.

Serves 4 to 6

Brown Rice with Mushrooms

Great served with grilled chicken or other vegetables.

2 shallots, chopped
2 tablespoons butter
8 ounces fresh mushrooms,
    chopped
6 cups hot cooked brown rice
2 tablespoons soy sauce
1 tablespoon white wine vinegar
1 cup coarsely chopped walnuts

- Sauté the shallots in the butter in a skillet until tender. Add the mushrooms. Sauté until tender.

- Combine the brown rice, sautéed vegetables, soy sauce and white wine vinegar in a bowl and mix well. Add the walnuts just before serving.

Serves 5 or 6

Parslied Rice

1 medium onion, chopped
2 garlic cloves, minced
1 tablespoon vegetable oil
4 cups water
2 cups uncooked long grain rice
4 chicken bouillon cubes
3 tablespoons lemon juice
1/2 cup chopped fresh parsley

- Sauté the onion and garlic in the oil in a large saucepan until tender. Add the water, rice, bouillon cubes and lemon juice and mix well.

- Bring to a boil and reduce the heat. Simmer, covered, for 20 minutes or until the rice is tender and the liquid has been absorbed.

- Stir in the parsley.

- Note: You may substitute 4 cups chicken broth for the bouillon cubes and water.

Serves 8

Sage Dressing

This recipe has been in our family for years and we always prepare it every Thanksgiving.
Just add freshly made cranberry sauce and gravy—oh, how good.

1 1/2 cups finely chopped onion
1 1/2 cups finely chopped celery
1/3 cup butter
8 cups crumbled corn bread
1 1/2 teaspoons salt
1/8 teaspoon pepper
1/2 teaspoon poultry seasoning
1/2 teaspoon sage
1/4 cup water
1 egg, well beaten

- Preheat the oven to 350 degrees.

- Sauté the onion and celery in the butter in a large Dutch oven until tender. Add the corn bread, salt, pepper, poultry seasoning, sage, water and egg and mix well.

- Spoon into a large greased baking dish.

- Bake for 30 minutes or until brown.

Serves 8 to 10 or makes enough to stuff a 10-pound turkey

Garlic Butter

1 garlic bulb
2 tablespoons olive oil
2 tablespoons fresh lemon juice
1 1/2 teaspoons grated lemon zest
1/2 teaspoon pepper
1 sprig of fresh rosemary
1 sprig of fresh thyme
1 cup (2 sticks) butter, softened

- Preheat the oven to 425 degrees.

- Cut off the pointed end of the garlic bulb. Place on a piece of foil. Drizzle with the olive oil and lemon juice. Sprinkle with the lemon zest and pepper. Top with the rosemary and thyme sprigs. Fold the foil to seal.

- Bake for 30 minutes. Remove from the oven to cool.

- Squeeze the pulp from the garlic cloves into a medium bowl. Add the butter and mash well.

- Chill, covered, for 8 hours.

- Serve with potatoes, bread slices or fish.

Makes 1 cup

Sweets

My child, eat
honey because it is good.
Honey from the
honeycomb tastes sweet.
In the same way,
wisdom is pleasing to you.
If you find it,
you have hope for the
future, and your
wishes will come true.

Proverbs 24:13
New Century Version

Brandy Snaps

Cookies:
1/2 cup packed brown sugar
1/3 cup butter, melted
1/4 cup light molasses
1 tablespoon brandy
3/4 cup flour
1/2 teaspoon ginger
1/2 teaspoon nutmeg

Cream Filling:
2 cups whipping cream
1/4 cup confectioners' sugar,
  sifted
2 tablespoons brandy

- Preheat the oven to 350 degrees.

- For the cookies, combine the brown sugar, butter, molasses and 1 tablespoon brandy in a large bowl and mix well. Add the flour, ginger and nutmeg and mix well.

- Drop the batter by teaspoonfuls 3 inches apart onto greased cookie sheets allowing only 5 cookies per sheet.

- Bake for 5 to 6 minutes or until bubbly and a deep golden brown. Cool on the cookie sheets until the cookies have set. Remove the cookies quickly 1 at a time, placing each upside down on a heatproof surface. Roll each cookie around a metal cone or a greased handle of a wooden spoon. Let stand until firm. Slide the cookies off the cone or handle onto a wire rack to cool completely. Reheat in the oven for 1 minute if the cookies harden before shaping.

- For the cream filling, combine the whipping cream, confectioners' sugar and 2 tablespoons brandy in a chilled mixing bowl. Beat with chilled beaters until stiff peaks form.

- Spoon the filling into a pastry bag fitted with a large star tip. Pipe into the cookies.

Makes 54 cookies

We may give without loving,
but we cannot love without giving.

Bourbon Brownies

Super good.

1 package family-size brownie mix
1 cup chopped pecans
1/3 cup bourbon
1/2 cup (1 stick) butter, softened
1 1/2 teaspoons almond extract
2 cups sifted confectioners' sugar
2 cups (12 ounces) chocolate chips
1 tablespoon shortening

- Preheat the oven to 350 degrees.

- Prepare the brownie mix using the package directions. Add the pecans. Pour into a 10×15-inch baking pan.

- Bake for 20 minutes. Pour the bourbon over the hot brownies. Chill, covered, in the refrigerator.

- Cream the butter, almond extract and confectioners' sugar in a mixing bowl until smooth. Spread over the chilled brownies. Chill, covered, in the refrigerator.

- Melt the chocolate chips and shortening in a double boiler. Spread over the brownies. Let stand until set. Cut into bars or squares.

Makes 6 dozen

Cappuccino Brownies

5 1/3 cups (2 pounds) milk
    chocolate chips
1/4 cup instant coffee granules
1 cup (2 sticks) unsalted butter,
    softened
2 cups sugar
8 eggs
3 tablespoons vanilla extract
1 teaspoon cinnamon
1 teaspoon salt
2 cups flour

- Preheat the oven to 375 degrees.

- Combine the chocolate chips and coffee granules in a double boiler. Cook over simmering water over medium heat until the chocolate melts, stirring occasionally.

- Beat the butter in a mixing bowl until fluffy. Add the sugar gradually, beating constantly. Beat in the eggs 2 at a time. Continue to beat for 3 minutes or until the mixture is pale yellow. Add the vanilla, cinnamon and salt and mix well. Beat in the chocolate mixture. Add the flour and beat until smooth and creamy. Spoon into 4 lightly greased and floured 8-×8-inch baking pans.

- Bake for 35 minutes or until the edges pull from the sides of the pans. Cool in the pans on wire racks.

- Chill, covered, for 8 to 12 hours. Cut into bars to serve.

Makes 6 1/2 dozen

Incredible Brownies

3/4 cup packed brown sugar
1/2 cup (1 stick) unsalted butter,
    softened
1 teaspoon vanilla extract
1/4 teaspoon salt
2 eggs
3/4 cup Ghirardelli ground
    chocolate
1/2 cup flour
1/2 cup (3 ounces) chocolate chips
1/2 cup (3 ounces) white chocolate
    chips
1/2 cup chopped pecans

• Preheat the oven to 350 degrees.

• Beat the brown sugar, butter, vanilla and salt in a mixing bowl until creamy. Add the eggs 1 at a time, beating well after each addition. Add the chocolate and mix until blended. Stir in the flour, chocolate chips, white chocolate chips and pecans. Spoon into an 8×8-inch baking pan.

• Bake for 25 to 35 minutes or until the edges pull from the side of the pan. Cool in the pan on a wire rack. Cut into squares.

Makes 20

Cherry Chocolate Chip Cookies

2 cups flour
2 teaspoons baking soda
1/2 teaspoon baking powder
2 teaspoons salt
1 cup (2 sticks) butter, softened
1/2 cup packed light brown sugar
2 eggs
1/4 cup vanilla extract
1 1/2 cups chopped dried cherries
1 1/2 cups chopped pecans
3 1/2 cups (21 ounces) semisweet
    chocolate chips

• Preheat the oven to 350 degrees.

• Mix the flour, baking soda, baking powder and salt together.

• Cream the butter and brown sugar in a large mixing bowl until light and fluffy. Add the eggs and vanilla and mix well. Add the dried cherries and mix well. Add the flour mixture gradually, beating well after each addition. Fold in the pecans and chocolate chips.

• Drop by teaspoonfuls 2 inches apart onto greased cookie sheets.

• Bake for 10 to 15 minutes. Remove cookies immediately to wire racks to cool. Store in an airtight container.

Makes 4 to 5 dozen

The Chip Chip Cookie

2 1/2 cups rolled oats
2 cups flour
1/2 teaspoon salt
1 teaspoon baking powder
1 teaspoon baking soda
1 cup (2 sticks) butter, softened
1 cup sugar
1 cup packed brown sugar
2 eggs
1 teaspoon vanilla extract
2 cups (12 ounces) white
    chocolate chips
2 cups (12 ounces) semisweet
    chocolate chips
1 cup chopped nuts

- Preheat the oven to 375 degrees.

- Process the oats in a food processor to a powder. Mix the processed oats, flour, salt, baking powder and baking soda together.

- Cream the butter, sugar and brown sugar in a mixing bowl until light and fluffy. Add the eggs and vanilla and beat well. Add the flour mixture and mix well. Stir in the white chocolate chips, chocolate chips and nuts.

- Drop by golf ball-size portions 2 inches apart onto ungreased cookie sheets.

- Bake for 8 to 10 minutes. Cool on wire racks.

Makes about 5 dozen

Chocolate Softies

1 (2-layer) package Duncan Hines
    devil's food cake mix
1/3 cup water
1/4 cup (1/2 stick) butter, softened
1 egg
1 cup (12 ounces) white chocolate
    chips
1/2 cup coarsely chopped walnuts

- Preheat the oven to 350 degrees.

- Combine the cake mix, water, butter and egg in a large mixing bowl and beat at low speed until moistened. Beat at medium speed for 1 minute. The batter will be thick. Stir in the white chocolate chips and walnuts.

- Drop by heaping teaspoonfuls 2 inches apart onto greased cookie sheets.

- Bake for 10 to 12 minutes or until brown. Cool on the cookie sheets for 1 minute. Remove to wire racks to cool completely.

Makes about 4 dozen

Iced Chocolate Cookies

Cookies:
1 cup sugar
3/4 cup (1 1/2 sticks) butter, melted
1 egg
6 tablespoons baking cocoa
1/2 cup milk
1 teaspoon vanilla extract
2 cups flour
1/2 teaspoon baking soda
1/2 teaspoon salt
1 cup walnuts, chopped

Chocolate Frosting:
2 tablespoons butter
2 tablespoons milk
3 tablespoons baking cocoa
2 cups confectioners' sugar
1 teaspoon vanilla extract

- Preheat the oven to 375 degrees.

- For the cookies, combine the sugar, 3/4 cup butter, egg, 6 tablespoons baking cocoa, 1/2 cup milk and 1 teaspoon vanilla in a mixing bowl and mix well. Stir in the flour, baking soda, salt and walnuts.

- Drop by teaspoonfuls 2 inches apart onto greased cookie sheets.

- Bake for 8 to 10 minutes or until firm. Remove to wire racks to cool.

- For the frosting, melt 2 tablespoons butter with 2 tablespoons milk in a small saucepan over medium heat. Remove from the heat. Stir in 3 tablespoons baking cocoa and the confectioners' sugar. Beat until smooth, adding additional milk if needed for the desired consistency. Stir in 1 teaspoon vanilla.

- Spread the frosting over the cooled cookies.

Makes about 4 dozen

The most important things in life aren't things.

Iced Lemon Cookies

These cookies make nice afternoon snacks and are great served with fresh fruit.

Cookies:
2 2/3 cups flour
1/2 teaspoon baking powder
1 teaspoon baking soda
1/2 teaspoon salt
1/2 cup (1 stick) butter, softened
1 1/2 cups sugar
2 eggs
1 cup light sour cream
1 teaspoon grated lemon zest
1 tablespoon lemon juice

Lemon Frosting:
6 tablespoons butter
1 1/2 cups confectioners' sugar
1 tablespoon lemon juice
1/2 teaspoon vanilla extract

- Preheat the oven to 375 degrees.

- For the cookies, mix the flour, baking powder, baking soda and salt together.

- Cream 1/2 cup butter and the sugar in a mixing bowl until fluffy. Add the eggs 1 at a time, beating well after each addition. Add the flour mixture and sour cream alternately 1/3 at a time, beating well after each addition. Stir in the lemon zest and 1 tablespoon lemon juice.

- Drop by teaspoonfuls 1 1/2 inches apart onto well-greased cookie sheets.

- Bake for 10 minutes or until light brown. Remove to wire racks to cool.

- For the lemon frosting, melt 6 tablespoons butter in a saucepan. Stir in the confectioners' sugar, 1 tablespoon lemon juice and vanilla. Add just enough water to create a spreading consistency.

- Spread the frosting over the cookies.

Makes about 4 dozen

Iced Oatmeal Cookies

Cookies:
2 cups flour
1 1/2 teaspoons baking soda
2 teaspoons cinnamon
1/2 teaspoon salt
1 cup (2 sticks) butter, softened
2 cups sugar
2 eggs
1 1/2 tablespoons honey
1 teaspoon vanilla extract
2 cups quick-cooking oats

Confectioners' Sugar Glaze:
1 cup confectioners' sugar
2 tablespoons milk

- Preheat the oven to 350 degrees.

- For the cookies, mix the flour, baking soda, cinnamon and salt together.

- Cream the butter and sugar in a mixing bowl until light and fluffy. Add the eggs, honey and vanilla and mix well. Add the flour mixture gradually, beating constantly. Stir in the oats.

- Drop by teaspoonfuls 2 inches apart onto ungreased cookie sheets.

- Bake for 6 to 7 minutes or until golden brown. Remove to wire racks to cool for a few minutes.

- For the confectioners' sugar glaze, mix the confectioners' sugar and milk in a small bowl until smooth.

- Spread the glaze on the warm cookies.

Makes about 5 dozen

White Chocolate Oatmeal Cookies

3/4 cup raisins
3 tablespoons orange juice
1 cup flour
1 teaspoon baking soda
1/2 cup (1 stick) butter, softened
3/4 cup sugar
1 egg
2 teaspoons grated orange zest
1 1/2 cups rolled oats
1 1/2 cups white chocolate chips

- Combine the raisins and orange juice in a bowl. Chill, covered, for 8 to 12 hours.

- Preheat the oven to 350 degrees.

- Mix the flour and baking soda together.

- Cream the butter and sugar in a large mixing bowl until light and fluffy. Beat in the egg and orange zest. Add the flour mixture and mix well. Add the raisin mixture, oats and white chocolate chips and mix well.

- Drop by rounded teaspoonfuls 2 inches apart onto greased cookie sheets and flatten slightly.

- Bake for 8 to 10 minutes or until golden brown. Cool on the cookie sheets for 1 minute. Remove to wire racks to cool completely.

Makes 3 dozen

Tea Cakes

3 cups flour
2 teaspoons baking powder
1/4 teaspoon salt
1/2 cup (1 stick) butter, softened
3/4 cup plus 1 tablespoon sugar
2 eggs, beaten
1 teaspoon vanilla extract
1/4 cup sugar
1/4 teaspoon nutmeg

- Preheat the oven to 375 degrees.

- Mix the flour, baking powder and salt in a bowl with a whisk.

- Cream the butter in a mixing bowl. Add 3/4 cup plus 1 tablespoon sugar gradually, beating constantly until light and fluffy. Add the eggs and vanilla and mix well. Beat in the flour mixture to form a soft dough.

- Roll the dough into a thin circle on a lightly floured surface. Cut into circles with a cookie cutter. Sprinkle with a mixture of 1/4 cup sugar and nutmeg. Arrange 2 inches apart on lightly greased baking sheets.

- Bake for 8 to 10 minutes or until golden brown. Cool on wire racks.

Makes 6 dozen

White Chocolate Nut Bars

2 cups flour
1 teaspoon baking soda
1 teaspoon salt
1/2 cup (1 stick) butter, softened
1 cup packed brown sugar
1/2 cup sugar
2 eggs
1 1/2 teaspoons vanilla extract
1 cup chopped macadamia nuts
2 cups (24 ounces) white
    chocolate chips

- Preheat the oven to 350 degrees.

- Mix the flour, baking soda and salt together.

- Cream the butter, brown sugar and sugar in a mixing bowl until light and fluffy. Add the eggs and vanilla and mix well. Beat in the flour mixture. Stir in the macadamia nuts and white chocolate chips.

- Spread the batter in a greased 9×13-inch baking pan.

- Bake for 30 to 35 minutes or until the edges pull from the side of the pan. Let stand until cool. Cut into bars.

Makes 2 1/2 dozen

Black Mocha Cake

Cake:
1³/4 cups flour
2 teaspoons baking soda
1 teaspoon baking powder
1 teaspoon salt
2 cups sugar
³/4 cup baking cocoa
2 eggs
1 cup strong black coffee
1 cup buttermilk
¹/2 cup vegetable oil
1 teaspoon vanilla extract

Caramel Fluff:
2 cups whipping cream
³/4 cup packed brown sugar
1 teaspoon vanilla extract

- Preheat the oven to 350 degrees.

- For the cake, mix the flour, baking soda, baking powder, salt, sugar and baking cocoa in a large mixing bowl. Add the eggs, coffee, buttermilk, oil and 1 teaspoon vanilla. Beat at medium speed for 2 minutes. The batter will be thin.

- Pour into a greased and floured bundt pan.

- Bake for 30 to 40 minutes or until the cake tests done. Cool in the pan for 10 minutes. Invert the cake onto a wire rack to cool completely.

- For the caramel fluff, beat the whipping cream, brown sugar and 1 teaspoon vanilla in a chilled mixing bowl until stiff peaks form.

- To serve, cut the cake into slices and place on serving plates. Dollop with caramel fluff. Garnish with shaved chocolate.

Serves 16

Easy Chocolate Cake

Cake:
1 (2-layer) package yellow cake mix
1 (6-ounce) package chocolate instant pudding mix
4 eggs
1 cup vegetable oil
¹/2 cup vodka
¹/2 cup water
¹/2 cup sugar
¹/4 cup Kahlúa

Kahlúa Glaze:
¹/4 cup Kahlúa
¹/2 cup confectioners' sugar

- Preheat the oven to 350 degrees.

- For the cake, beat the cake mix, pudding mix, eggs, oil, vodka, water, sugar and ¹/4 cup Kahlúa at medium speed in a mixing bowl until smooth. Pour into a greased and floured bundt pan.

- Bake for 50 minutes. Cool in the pan slightly. Invert onto a cake plate.

- For the Kahlúa glaze, mix ¹/4 cup Kahlúa and confectioners' sugar in a bowl until smooth.

- Puncture the warm cake surface with a large wooden pick. Brush with the glaze. Let cool until the glaze hardens.

Serves 16

Chocolate Muffin Cakes

Sugar
1/2 cup (1 stick) unsalted butter,
   cut into pieces
5 ounces bittersweet chocolate,
   coarsely chopped
4 egg yolks
2 tablespoons sugar
2 egg whites
2 tablespoons sugar
1 pint coffee ice cream

- Preheat the oven to 350 degrees.

- Grease 4 cups in a jumbo nonstick muffin pan, leaving the 2 center cups empty. Coat lightly with sugar.

- Melt the butter and chocolate in a bowl over simmering water, stirring constantly. Remove from the heat.

- Beat the egg yolks and 2 tablespoons sugar with a whisk in a mixing bowl until thick and pale yellow. Stir in the chocolate mixture.

- Beat the egg whites in a mixing bowl until soft peaks form. Add 2 tablespoons sugar gradually, beating constantly until stiff peaks form. Fold into the chocolate mixture. Spoon into the prepared muffin cups.

- Bake for 25 minutes or until set and slightly springy to the touch. Cool in the pan for 15 minutes.

- Run a knife carefully around the edge of the cakes and unmold. Serve each with a scoop of the coffee ice cream. Drizzle with Kahlúa chocolate sauce, if desired.

Serves 4

Easy Cherry Cake

1/2 cup (1 stick) butter
2 eggs
1 (2-layer) package yellow cake
  mix
1 (20-ounce) can cherry pie filling
8 ounces cream cheese, softened
2 eggs
1 (1-pound) package
  confectioners' sugar

- Preheat the oven to 350 degrees.

- Melt the butter in a 9×13-inch cake pan.

- Beat 2 eggs and the cake mix at medium speed in a mixing bowl until smooth. Spread over the butter. Spread the pie filling over the batter.

- Beat the cream cheese and 2 eggs at medium speed in a mixing bowl until smooth and creamy. Add the confectioners' sugar and beat well. Spread over the pie filling.

- Bake for 40 to 50 minutes or until golden brown.

Serves 15

*One good thing about being wrong
is the joy it brings to others.*

Gingerbread with Lemon Fondue

Gingerbread:
2 1/2 cups flour
1 1/2 teaspoons baking soda
1/2 teaspoon salt
1 teaspoon ginger
1 teaspoon cinnamon
1/2 teaspoon cloves
1/2 cup (1 stick) butter, softened
1/2 cup sugar
1 egg
1 cup molasses
1 cup water

Lemon Fondue:
4 1/2 cups water
3 cups confectioners' sugar
2/3 cup cornstarch
1/4 cup grated lemon zest
1 1/2 cups (3 sticks) butter
2 (6-ounce) cans frozen
    lemonade concentrate,
    thawed

- Preheat the oven to 350 degrees.

- For the gingerbread, mix the flour, baking soda, salt, ginger, cinnamon and cloves together.

- Cream 1/2 cup butter and sugar in a large mixing bowl until light and fluffy. Add the egg and molasses. Add the flour mixture gradually, beating constantly. Add 1 cup water and beat well. Pour into a greased 9×13-inch cake pan.

- Bake for 30 to 40 minutes or until the gingerbread tests done. Cool in the pan.

- For the lemon fondue, combine 4 1/2 cups water, confectioners' sugar, cornstarch and lemon zest in a medium saucepan and stir until the cornstarch is dissolved. Add 1 1/2 cups butter.

- Cook over low heat until the butter melts and the sauce is thickened, stirring constantly. Stir in the lemonade concentrate. Cook for 1 to 2 minutes or until heated through. Pour into a fondue pot to keep warm.

- To serve, cut the gingerbread into small cubes. Serve with the lemon fondue.

Serves 15

Jam Cake

Cake:
1 cup buttermilk
1 teaspoon baking soda
1 teaspoon baking powder
1/2 cup boiling water
2 eggs, beaten
2 cups sugar
2/3 cup shortening
1 cup raisins
1 cup blackberry jam
1 cup applesauce
1 cup pecans, chopped
3 cups flour
1/2 cup baking cocoa
1 teaspoon cinnamon
1 teaspoon allspice
1 teaspoon nutmeg

Brown Sugar Frosting:
1/4 cup shortening
1/4 cup (1/2 stick) butter
2 cups sugar
1 cup milk
1/2 cup sugar
1 teaspoon vanilla extract

- Preheat the oven to 350 degrees.

- For the cake, combine the buttermilk, baking soda, baking powder and boiling water in a large bowl and blend well.

- Beat the eggs, 2 cups sugar and 2/3 cup shortening in a large mixing bowl until light and fluffy. Add the buttermilk mixture and beat well. Fold in the raisins, jam, applesauce and pecans. Stir in the flour, baking cocoa, cinnamon, allspice and nutmeg. Spoon into 3 lightly oiled and floured 9-inch cake pans.

- Bake for 30 to 35 minutes or until the layers test done. Cool in the pans for 10 minutes. Invert onto wire racks to cool completely.

- For the frosting, combine 1/4 cup shortening, butter, 2 cups sugar and the milk in a saucepan and mix well. Bring to a boil, stirring frequently.

- Brown 1/2 cup sugar in a medium saucepan, stirring constantly to prevent burning. Stir into the shortening mixture. Add the vanilla and mix well.

- To serve, spread the frosting between the layers and over the top and side of the cake.

Serves 10

Peach Cake

3 cups flour
3/4 teaspoon salt
1/4 teaspoon baking soda
2 cups peaches, peeled, chopped
1/2 cup sour cream
1 cup (2 sticks) butter, softened
3 cups sugar
6 eggs
1 teaspoon vanilla extract
1 teaspoon almond extract

- Preheat the oven to 350 degrees.

- Mix the flour, salt and baking soda together.

- Combine the peaches and sour cream in a bowl and mix well.

- Cream the butter and sugar in a mixing bowl until light and fluffy. Add the eggs 1 at a time, beating well after each addition. Add the flour mixture alternately with the peach mixture, beginning and ending with the flour mixture and beating well after each addition. Stir in the vanilla and almond extracts. Spoon into a greased and floured 10-inch tube pan.

- Bake for 75 to 80 minutes or until the cake tests done.

Serves 16

Peaches and Cream Cake

1 (2-layer) package butter-flavor
  cake mix
1 1/2 cups sugar
1/4 cup cornstarch
4 cups chopped fresh peaches
1/2 cup water
2 cups whipping cream
2 to 3 tablespoons confectioners'
  sugar
1 cup sour cream

- Prepare and bake the cake mix using the package directions for two 8-inch cake pans. Cool the layers. Cut each layer horizontally into halves.

- Mix the sugar and cornstarch in a saucepan. Add the peaches and water. Cook until smooth and thickened, stirring constantly. Remove from the heat. Let stand until cool.

- Beat the whipping cream and confectioners' sugar in a medium mixing bowl until stiff peaks form.

- To assemble, arrange 1 cake layer on a cake platter. Spread 1/3 of the peach filling over the layer. Spread 1/3 cup sour cream over the filling. Top with another cake layer. Repeat the layers with the remaining peach filling, sour cream and cake layers, ending with a cake layer. Spread the whipped cream mixture over the top and side of the cake. Garnish with peach slices. Chill, covered, until ready to serve.

Serves 16

Lemon Roulade

For a nice touch, decorate with violets or mint leaves.

Cake:
2/3 cup sifted cake flour
1 teaspoon baking powder
1/4 teaspoon salt
4 egg yolks
1/2 cup sugar
1 teaspoon lemon extract
1/4 teaspoon almond extract
1/4 teaspoon coconut extract
1/4 teaspoon orange extract
1 tablespoon vegetable oil
4 egg whites
1/4 cup sugar
Confectioners' sugar

Lemon Filling:
1 (14-ounce) can sweetened
    condensed milk
1/3 cup fresh lemon juice
1 teaspoon grated lemon zest
4 ounces whipped topping

- Preheat the oven to 375 degrees.

- For the cake, grease a 10×15-inch jelly roll pan and line with waxed paper.

- Mix the cake flour, baking powder and salt together.

- Whisk the egg yolks in a mixing bowl until pale yellow. Add 1/2 cup sugar gradually, beating constantly. Stir in the flavorings and oil.

- Beat the egg whites in a mixing bowl until foamy. Add 1/4 cup sugar gradually, beating constantly until stiff peaks form. Fold into the egg yolk mixture. Fold in the cake flour mixture. Spread evenly in the prepared jelly roll pan.

- Bake for 10 to 15 minutes or until golden brown. Sift confectioners' sugar on a 10×15-inch linen towel. Invert the hot cake onto the prepared towel and remove the waxed paper. Roll up the cake in the towel beginning at the narrow end. Cool seam side down on a wire rack.

- For the lemon filling, combine the condensed milk, lemon juice and lemon zest in a bowl and blend well. Fold in the whipped topping.

- To assemble, unroll the cake. Spread with 1/2 of the lemon filling. Reroll the cake. Arrange seam side down on a serving platter. Spread the remaining lemon filling over the cake. Chill, covered, for 1 to 2 hours before serving.

Serves 8 to 10

Raspberry Roulade

Cake:

1 cup chopped semisweet
    chocolate
3 tablespoons hot water
5 egg yolks, beaten
3/4 cup sugar
1 teaspoon vanilla extract
5 egg whites, stiffly beaten
Baking cocoa
1/2 cup seedless raspberry jam
2 tablespoons framboise
3 cups whipping cream
1/4 cup sugar

Raspberry Sauce:

4 cups fresh or frozen
    unsweetened raspberries
1 cup sugar, or to taste
3 to 4 tablespoons fresh lemon
    juice

- Preheat the oven to 300 degrees.

- For the cake, line a 10×15-inch jelly roll pan with waxed paper. Grease the waxed paper.

- Heat the chocolate in the hot water in a double boiler until the chocolate melts.

- Beat the egg yolks and 3/4 cup sugar in a mixing bowl. Stir in the melted chocolate and vanilla. Fold in the stiffly beaten egg whites. Spoon into the prepared jelly roll pan.

- Bake for 20 to 25 minutes or until the cake tests done. Remove the pan from the oven. Place a damp cloth over the cake. Let stand for 5 minutes.

- Sprinkle a 16-inch piece of foil generously with baking cocoa. Invert the cake onto the foil. Score the cake about every inch; do not cut through the cake. This will help in rolling the cake.

- Blend the raspberry jam and framboise in a small bowl. Spread a thin layer over the cake to the edges. Beat the whipping cream and 1/4 cup sugar in a mixing bowl until soft peaks form. Spread over the jam layer. Roll as for a jelly roll. Wrap the cake tightly in foil. Chill for 8 hours.

- For the raspberry sauce, purée the raspberries, 1/2 cup of the sugar and 3 tablespoons lemon juice in a food processor or blender for 2 to 3 minutes or until the sugar is completely dissolved. Add the remaining sugar by spoonfuls and the remaining lemon juice gradually if needed, processing constantly. Strain into a bowl. Chill, covered, in the refrigerator.

- To serve, cut the cake roll into slices and serve with the raspberry sauce.

Serves 6 to 8

White Chocolate Cake

Cake:
1 cup (2 sticks) butter, softened
2 cups sugar
4 eggs
1 teaspoon vanilla extract
1 1/2 cups flour
1 teaspoon baking powder
1 cup buttermilk
1 cup chopped pecans
8 ounces white chocolate, melted

Butter Frosting:
1 cup shortening
1/2 cup (1 stick) butter, softened
1 (2-pound) package
   confectioners' sugar, sifted
1/2 cup milk
1 1/2 teaspoons vanilla extract

- Preheat the oven to 350 degrees.

- For the cake, cream 1 cup butter in a mixing bowl. Add the sugar gradually, beating until light and fluffy. Add the eggs 1 at a time, beating well after each addition. Beat in 1 teaspoon vanilla.

- Sift the flour and baking powder together. Add to the creamed mixture alternately with the buttermilk, beating well after each addition. Stir in the pecans and melted white chocolate.

- Pour into 3 greased and floured 8-inch cake pans or 2 greased and floured 9-inch cake pans. Bake for 30 minutes or until a wooden pick inserted in the center comes out clean. Cool in the pans for 5 minutes. Remove to wire racks to cool completely.

- For the frosting, beat the shortening and 1/2 cup butter in a mixing bowl until light and fluffy. Add the confectioners' sugar, milk and 1 1/2 teaspoons vanilla and beat until smooth.

- To assemble, spread the frosting between the layers and over the top and side of the cake.

Serves 10 to 12

Caramel Frosting

3 cups sugar
1 1/2 cups whipping cream
1/4 cup (1/2 stick) butter
1/4 teaspoon baking soda
3/4 cup sugar

- Bring 3 cups sugar, the whipping cream, butter and baking soda to a boil in a heavy saucepan, stirring constantly. Remove from the heat and keep warm.

- Sprinkle 3/4 cup sugar in a cast-iron skillet. Cook over medium heat until the sugar melts and the syrup is a light golden brown, stirring constantly. Add to the whipping cream mixture gradually, stirring constantly until smooth.

Makes enough to frost a 9-inch layer cake

Creamy Fudge Bottom Pie

Crust:
1 cup graham cracker crumbs
2 tablespoons confectioners' sugar
3 1/2 tablespoons melted butter

Pie:
1 cup heavy cream
8 ounces bittersweet chocolate, finely chopped
2 cups heavy cream
2 cups light cream
2 (3-ounce) packages vanilla instant pudding mix

- For the crust, mix the graham cracker crumbs, confectioners' sugar and butter in a bowl. Press into a 9-inch pie plate. Freeze in the freezer.

- For the pie, heat 1 cup heavy cream in a small saucepan until bubbles appear around the edge. Pour over the chocolate in a bowl. Let stand for 5 minutes. Whisk until smooth. Remove the crust from the freezer. Pour the chocolate mixture into the crust. Chill, covered, for 1 to 1 1/2 hours or until firm.

- Combine 2 cups heavy cream and the light cream in a large mixing bowl and blend well. Add the pudding mix and beat until thick and stiff. Spoon over the chocolate layer, mounding in the center. Freeze, uncovered, for 4 to 5 hours or until frozen through.

- To serve, thaw the pie partially in the refrigerator. Garnish with baking cocoa or chocolate shavings.

Serves 6 to 8

Real Lemon Pie

3/4 cup sugar
3 tablespoons cornstarch
4 egg yolks
Juice of 2 lemons
Pinch of salt
1 cup boiling water
1 tablespoon butter, melted
4 egg whites
1/4 cup sugar
1 baked (9-inch) deep-dish pie
   shell

- Preheat the oven to 300 degrees.

- Mix 3/4 cup sugar and the cornstarch in a bowl. Add the egg yolks and beat well. Add the lemon juice and salt and mix well.

- Combine the boiling water and butter in a double boiler. Stir in the lemon mixture. Cook until thickened, stirring constantly.

- Beat the egg whites in a mixing bowl until soft peaks form. Add 1/4 cup sugar gradually, beating constantly until stiff peaks form. Fold 1/2 of the meringue into the filling. Spoon into the baked pie shell. Top with the remaining meringue, spreading to the edge.

- Bake until the top is light brown.

Serves 8

Lemonade Pie

1 (6-ounce) can frozen lemonade
   concentrate, thawed
1 (14-ounce) can sweetened
   condensed milk
8 ounces whipped topping
1 (9-inch) graham cracker
   pie shell

- Combine the lemonade concentrate and condensed milk in a large bowl and mix well. Fold in the whipped topping. Spoon into the pie shell.

- Chill, covered, for 3 to 12 hours.

Serves 6 to 8

Strawberry Custard Pie

2/3 cup sugar
1/4 cup cornstarch
1/4 teaspoon salt
2 cups milk
2 egg yolks, lightly beaten
1 teaspoon vanilla extract
1 tablespoon butter
1 baked (9-inch) pie shell
2/3 cup sugar
3 tablespoons cornstarch
1 cup water
1 tablespoon lemon juice
1/2 teaspoon red food coloring
  (optional)
6 cups fresh strawberry halves

- Combine 2/3 cup sugar, 1/4 cup cornstarch and the salt in a saucepan. Stir in the milk. Bring to a boil. Cook for 1 minute, stirring constantly. Stir a small amount of the hot mixture into the egg yolks. Stir the egg yolks into the hot mixture.

- Cook over medium heat for 1 minute or until thickened, whisking constantly. Remove from the heat. Stir in the vanilla and butter. Spoon into the pie shell.

- Combine 2/3 cup sugar, 3 tablespoons cornstarch and 2 tablespoons of the water in a bowl. Bring the remaining water to a boil in a saucepan. Whisk in the sugar mixture. Cook for 2 to 3 minutes or until thickened and clear, whisking constantly. Stir in the lemon juice and food coloring. Remove from the heat to cool. Fold in the strawberries. Spoon over the custard mixture.

- Chill, covered, for 4 hours.

- Garnish with whipped cream and strawberries.

Serves 6 to 8

*Growing old is mandatory;
growing up is optional.*

Fruit Tarts

Nice for tea parties or a dessert tray.

1 recipe favorite pastry
³/4 cup strawberry or cherry
    preserves
2 eggs
¹/2 cup sugar
2 tablespoons flour
2 tablespoons melted butter
¹/2 cup ground almonds
Dash of nutmeg
1 teaspoon vanilla or almond
    extract

- Preheat the oven to 350 degrees.

- Line 24 miniature tart pans with pastry. Spoon the preserves into each.

- Beat the eggs lightly in a mixing bowl. Add a mixture of the sugar and flour and mix well. Add the butter, almonds, nutmeg and vanilla and mix well. Spoon into the prepared tart shells.

- Bake for 30 minutes or until the filling is set.

- Note: You may use miniature frozen pastry shells instead of the pastry.

Makes 2 dozen

A closed mouth gathers no feet.

Bread Pudding

Bread Pudding:
1/2 cup raisins
4 cups milk
1 1/2 cups sugar
1 cup whipping cream
4 eggs
1/2 cup chopped pecans
1 teaspoon cinnamon
1 teaspoon nutmeg
1 teaspoon vanilla extract
1 loaf dry French bread
6 tablespoons butter

Whiskey Sauce:
3 eggs
1 cup sugar
1/2 cup milk
1 teaspoon vanilla extract
1/4 cup cold water
1 tablespoon cornstarch
3 tablespoons whiskey

- Preheat the oven to 350 degrees.

- For the bread pudding, combine the raisins with enough warm water to cover in a bowl. Let stand for 2 hours; drain.

- Combine 4 cups milk, 1 1/2 cups sugar, the whipping cream and 4 eggs in a large mixing bowl and whisk until blended. Stir in the pecans and raisins. Add the cinnamon, nutmeg and 1 teaspoon vanilla and mix well.

- Tear the bread into small pieces. Add to the milk mixture and stir until moistened. Spoon into a buttered 9×13-inch baking dish. Dot with the butter.

- Place the dish in a larger baking dish. Add enough water to the larger dish to fill to a depth of 1/2 inch.

- Bake for 30 minutes. Remove from the water bath. Bake for 45 minutes longer.

- For the whiskey sauce, beat 3 eggs in a double boiler. Cook over medium heat until slightly thickened, whisking constantly. Stir in 1 cup sugar, 1/2 cup milk and 1 teaspoon vanilla. Cook until heated through, stirring frequently. Do not boil. Stir in a mixture of the cold water and cornstarch. Add the whiskey and mix well.

- Cook over medium heat for 15 minutes or until thickened, stirring frequently.

- Serve the sauce chilled or at room temperature over the bread pudding.

Serves 15 to 18

Peach Bread Pudding

Bread Pudding:
1 loaf French bread
3/4 cup sugar
1/2 cup raisins (optional)
1/2 teaspoon nutmeg
1 teaspoon cinnamon
1/2 teaspoon cloves
1/2 teaspoon salt
3 cups milk, scalded
1/2 cup (1 stick) butter, melted
1/2 teaspoon vanilla extract
4 eggs, beaten
2 cups chopped fresh peaches,
    cooked, drained

Whiskey Sauce:
5 egg yolks
1/4 cup sugar
Dash of cloves
1/4 cup whiskey
1/4 cup (1/2 stick) butter, melted
1/4 teaspoon vanilla extract
1/3 cup heavy cream

Chantilly Cream:
1 cup heavy cream
1/4 cup sugar
1/2 teaspoon vanilla extract
1 teaspoon brandy
1 teaspoon triple sec
1 1/2 tablespoons sour cream

- Preheat the oven to 350 degrees.

- For the bread pudding, tear the bread into 1-inch cubes into a large mixing bowl. Add 3/4 cup sugar, the raisins, nutmeg, cinnamon, 1/2 teaspoon cloves and salt. Stir in the milk and butter. Add 1/2 teaspoon vanilla, the eggs and peaches and mix well. Pour into a greased baking pan.

- Bake for 45 minutes.

- For the whiskey sauce, combine the egg yolks, 1/4 cup sugar, dash of cloves and whiskey in a saucepan. Cook over medium heat until the mixture doubles and thickens, stirring constantly with a whisk. Remove from the heat. Add 1/4 cup butter and 1/4 teaspoon vanilla gradually, beating constantly. Stir in 1/3 cup heavy cream gradually.

- For the chantilly cream, beat 1 cup heavy cream and 1/4 cup sugar in a mixing bowl until stiff peaks form. Fold in 1/2 teaspoon vanilla, the brandy, triple sec and sour cream using a spatula.

- To serve, spoon the bread pudding into serving bowls. Top with the whiskey sauce and chantilly cream.

Serves 8

Kahlúa Chocolate Ice Cream Torte

1/2 cup (1 stick) butter
1/2 cup chopped walnuts or
    almonds
1 cup flour
1/2 cup sugar
1 cup whipping cream, whipped
1/4 cup Kahlúa
2 tablespoons strong coffee
1 quart chocolate ice cream,
    softened

- Melt the butter in a large skillet over medium heat. Add the walnuts, flour and sugar. Cook until the mixture is golden and crumbly, stirring constantly.

- Reserve 3/4 cup of the mixture for the topping. Press the remaining mixture into a 9-inch springform pan.

- Freeze, covered, for 4 hours or longer.

- Combine the whipped cream, Kahlúa, coffee and ice cream in a large mixing bowl and beat until smooth. Spoon immediately into the prepared pan.

- Freeze for 2 hours or until almost set. Sprinkle with the reserved crumb mixture. Cover and return to the freezer. Freeze for 2 to 12 hours or until firm.

- Cut into wedges to serve.

Serves 8

*Oh Lord, help me to keep my big mouth shut
until I know what I'm talking about.*

Refreshing Strawberry Ice Cream Torte

5 whole graham crackers, broken
   up
1/3 cup hazelnuts, toasted
1 tablespoon sugar
1/8 teaspoon salt
5 tablespoons unsalted butter,
   melted
4 pints vanilla ice cream
2 pints strawberry sorbet
2 1/2 pounds strawberries, sliced
1/3 cup sugar
Caramel Sauce (optional)
   (page 163)

- Preheat the oven to 350 degrees.

- Process the graham crackers, hazelnuts, 1 tablespoon sugar and the salt in a blender until the hazelnuts are finely chopped. Add the butter and process until the mixture is evenly moist.

- Press over the bottom of a 10-inch springform pan.

- Bake for 8 minutes or until golden brown. Remove from the oven and cool completely.

- Soften 1 1/4 pints of the ice cream. Spread over the crust. Freeze for 1 hour or until firm.

- Soften 1 pint of the sorbet. Spread over the ice cream layer. Freeze for 30 minutes or until firm.

- Soften 1 1/4 pints of the remaining ice cream. Spread over the sorbet layer. Freeze for 1 hour or until firm.

- Soften the remaining 1 pint of sorbet. Spread over the ice cream layer. Freeze for 30 minutes or until firm.

- Soften the remaining 1 1/2 pints of the ice cream. Spread over the top. Cover and freeze for 3 hours or up to 1 week.

- To serve, combine the strawberries and 1/3 cup sugar in a large bowl and stir to mix well. Let stand for 30 minutes or until the strawberries release their juices.

- Cut around the edge to loosen the ice cream cake from the side of the pan. Release the side. Cut into wedges. Spoon the strawberries over the top of each serving. Drizzle with Caramel Sauce (page 163), if desired.

Serves 16

Mississippi Pie Dessert

A favorite dessert.

Dessert:
1 cup flour
1/2 cup (1 stick) butter, softened
1/4 cup dark brown sugar
1/2 cup chopped pecans
1/2 gallon vanilla ice cream,
  softened

Caramel Sauce:
1/2 cup (1 stick) butter
1 1/2 cups dark brown sugar
1/8 teaspoon salt
2 tablespoons corn syrup
1/2 cup milk or half-and-half

- Preheat the oven to 375 degrees.

- For the dessert, mix the flour, 1/2 cup butter, 1/4 cup brown sugar and the pecans in a bowl. Spread in a buttered 9×13-inch baking pan.

- Bake for 15 minutes or until light brown. Remove from the oven to cool.

- Crumble the crust with a fork. Spread the ice cream over the crust. Freeze until firm.

- For the caramel sauce, combine 1/2 cup butter, 1 1/2 cups brown sugar, the salt, corn syrup and milk in a saucepan.

- Cook over medium heat for 15 minutes, stirring constantly. Remove from the heat. Cool to room temperature.

- Pour over the ice cream layer. Freeze until firm. Cut into squares.

Serves 12

Turkish Delight

1 package Duncan Hines brownie
  mix
1/2 gallon coffee ice cream,
  softened
1 jar caramel sauce
1 jar Mrs. Richardson's fudge
  sauce
Chopped pecans

- Prepare the brownie mix using the package directions. Pour into a well-greased 10-inch springform pan. Bake using the package directions. Cool in the pan.

- Spread the ice cream over the baked layer. Freeze until firm.

- Spoon a thin layer of caramel sauce over the ice cream layer. Freeze until firm.

- Spoon a thin layer of the fudge sauce over the top. Sprinkle with pecans. Freeze until ready to serve.

- To serve, remove the side of the pan. Cut into wedges. Drizzle each serving with the remaining caramel sauce.

Serves 10 to 12

Peaches with Raspberry Sauce

6 ripe peaches, peeled, cut into
    halves
Sugar
1/4 cup sweet sherry
2 (10-ounce) packages frozen
    raspberries, thawed
1 teaspoon cornstarch
2 tablespoons fresh lemon juice
1 quart pistachio ice cream

- Place the peaches in a bowl. Sprinkle with sugar. Drizzle with the sherry. Let stand for 30 minutes.

- Purée the raspberries in a blender. Strain into a saucepan, discarding the seeds. Bring to a boil. Dissolve the cornstarch in the lemon juice in a cup. Stir into the raspberry liquid.

- Cook until slightly thickened, stirring constantly. Remove from the heat to cool. Chill, covered, until ready to serve.

- To serve, place 2 peach halves in each sherbet dish. Add a scoop of the ice cream. Spoon the raspberry sauce over the top.

Serves 6

Spiced Peach Sundaes

1/4 cup (1/2 stick) unsalted butter
6 tablespoons dark brown sugar
1 teaspoon vanilla extract
1/2 teaspoon cardamom
1/8 teaspoon nutmeg
2 1/2 pounds ripe peaches, cut into
    slices 1/4 inch thick
1/2 gallon vanilla or caramel ice
    cream
Pecan halves, toasted
Sweetened whipped cream

- Melt the butter in a large heavy skillet over medium heat. Stir in the brown sugar. Add the vanilla, cardamom and nutmeg. Cook for 1 minute. Add the peaches and toss to coat. Cook for 5 minutes or until the brown sugar melts and the peaches are tender but do not fall apart.

- Place 2 scoops of ice cream into each serving bowl. Spoon the peach mixture over the ice cream. Sprinkle with pecan halves. Dollop with sweetened whipped cream.

Serves 8

White Chocolate Sundaes

Brownies:
10 ounces white chocolate,
  chopped
3/4 cup (1 1/2 sticks) unsalted
  butter
2 1/2 cups unbleached flour
1 teaspoon baking powder
1 teaspoon salt
6 eggs
2 cups sugar
1 tablespoon vanilla extract

Fudge Sauce:
1 cup whipping cream
1/4 cup fresh brewed coffee
Pinch of salt
1 teaspoon vanilla extract
1 pound bittersweet or semisweet
  chocolate, chopped

Raspberry Sauce:
1 (12-ounce) package frozen
  unsweetened raspberries,
  thawed
3 tablespoons sugar

Assembly:
Vanilla ice cream

- Preheat the oven to 350 degrees.

- For the brownies, line a 9×13-inch baking pan with foil, extending the foil over the sides. Butter the foil.

- Reserve 1/3 cup white chocolate. Melt the remaining white chocolate with the butter in a small saucepan over low heat until melted and smooth. Remove from the heat.

- Mix the flour, baking powder and 1 teaspoon salt in a medium bowl. Beat the eggs, 2 cups sugar and 1 tablespoon vanilla in a large bowl until fluffy. Stir in the white chocolate mixture. Fold in the flour mixture.

- Spread in the prepared pan. Sprinkle the reserved white chocolate over the batter.

- Bake for 45 minutes. Cool in the pan on a wire rack.

- For the fudge sauce, bring the whipping cream, coffee, pinch of salt and 1 teaspoon vanilla to a simmer in a heavy medium saucepan. Reduce the heat to low. Add the bittersweet chocolate. Whisk until melted and smooth.

- You may prepare the sauce up to 2 days ahead of serving and store, covered, in the refrigerator. Reheat over low heat before serving.

- For the raspberry sauce, purée the raspberries with 3 tablespoons sugar in a blender. Strain into a bowl, discarding the seeds.

- To assemble, cut the brownies into squares and place on serving plates. Top with ice cream. Drizzle with the raspberry sauce and fudge sauce. Garnish with whipped cream and walnuts. Serve immediately.

Serves 8

Lemon Ice Cream

2 cups sugar
2 cups milk
2 cups half-and-half
2 teaspoons grated lemon zest
1 cup lemon juice
6 drops of yellow food coloring
   (optional)

- Combine the sugar, milk, half-and-half, lemon zest, lemon juice and food coloring in a large bowl and blend well. Pour into a 9×13-inch pan.

- Freeze for 2 hours or longer.

- Process the frozen lemon mixture in a blender or food processor $1/2$ at a time until smooth. Return to the pan.

- Freeze for 4 hours or until firm.

- Garnish with fresh mint.

Makes 1 1/2 quarts

Cranberry Sorbet

A refreshing sorbet to cleanse the palate before the entrée is served.

1 (12-ounce) can frozen cranberry
   raspberry juice concentrate
1/2 cup orange juice
1 (16-ounce) can cranberry sauce
1/2 cup grapefruit juice
1/2 cup Sprite

- Combine the juice concentrate, orange juice, cranberry sauce, grapefruit juice and Sprite in a large bowl and mix well. Pour into a 9×11-inch glass dish. Cover with foil.

- Freeze for 6 to 12 hours or until almost solid.

- Spoon into a mixing bowl and beat until creamy. Spoon into a small bowl and cover tightly. Freeze until ready to serve.

- To serve, place 1 scoop sorbet into small sherbet cups or bowls. Garnish with raspberries and mint leaves.

Serves 8

Strawberry Sorbet

3 pints strawberries
2 cups sugar
1¹/2 cups orange juice
¹/4 cup lemon juice
¹/3 cup Grand Marnier (optional)

- Rinse the strawberries and hull. Place in a large bowl. Add the sugar, orange juice, lemon juice and Grand Marnier and toss to mix.

- Let stand at room temperature for 3 hours.

- Process in a blender until smooth. Pour into approximately 3 ice cube trays. Freeze until firm.

- Serve in cubes or process the cubes in a blender until slushy. Keep frozen until ready to serve.

Serves 8

Mixed Fruit Sauce

1 quart fresh strawberries, cut into
    halves
3 tablespoons sherry
1 teaspoon grated orange zest
¹/2 teaspoon grated lemon zest
2 tablespoons orange juice
2 teaspoons fresh lemon juice
2 tablespoons sugar
1 (10-ounce) package frozen
    raspberries, thawed
Vanilla ice cream

- Combine the strawberries, sherry, orange zest, lemon zest, orange juice, lemon juice and sugar in a large bowl and toss to mix well. Chill, covered, for 1 hour or longer.

- Purée the raspberries in a blender. Strain into a bowl, discarding the seeds. Chill, covered, in the refrigerator.

- To serve, combine the strawberry mixture and raspberry sauce in a bowl and mix well. Scoop vanilla ice cream into chilled individual sherbet dishes. Spoon the fruit sauce over the top.

Serves 6

Tropical Fruit Sauce

A wonderful sauce for fruit or cake, a light dessert or salad.

2 cups sour cream
3/4 cup packed brown sugar
1 teaspoon cinnamon
2/3 teaspoon nutmeg
1/4 cup brandy

- Process the sour cream, brown sugar, cinnamon, nutmeg and brandy in a blender.

- Serve over fresh fruit such as strawberries, kiwifruit or bananas.

Serves 4

Strawberry Sauce for Fresh Fruit

1 cup frozen unsweetened whole strawberries, thawed
2 teaspoons sugar
1/4 teaspoon grated orange zest
2 cups orange sections (about 6 oranges)
1 cup chopped peeled kiwifruit (about 3 kiwifruit)

- Process the strawberries, sugar and orange zest in a blender until smooth.

- Spoon 1/2 cup orange sections and 1/4 cup kiwifruit into each of 4 small bowls. Top each with 3 tablespoons of the strawberry sauce.

Serves 4

Special Strawberry Sauce

1 (10-ounce) package frozen strawberries, thawed
2 tablespoons sugar
1 tablespoon cornstarch
1/4 cup orange juice
1 1/4 cups sliced fresh strawberries
1 tablespoon Grand Marnier (optional)

- Purée the thawed undrained strawberries in a blender. Combine with the sugar, cornstarch and orange juice in a saucepan. Bring to a boil over medium-high heat. Cook for 4 minutes or until thickened, stirring constantly. Remove from the heat.

- Add the fresh strawberries and Grand Marnier and stir to mix well. Let cool to room temperature. Chill, covered, until ready to serve.

- Return to room temperature to serve. Serve over ice cream, pancakes, waffles, pound cake, etc.

Serves 6 to 8

Toffee Fudge Sauce

1 (14-ounce) package caramels
1/2 cup (3 ounces) chocolate chips
1/4 cup strong coffee
1/4 cup milk

- Unwrap the caramels and place in a heavy saucepan. Add the chocolate chips, coffee and milk.

- Cook over medium heat until melted, stirring occasionally.

Makes 2 cups

Index

PEACOCK PANTRY

Favorite Recipes from Peacock Hill Country Inn

Peacock Hill Counry Inn
6995 Giles Hill Road
College Grove, Tennessee 37046
1-800-327-6663

YOUR ORDER	QUANTITY	TOTAL
Peacock Pantry at $19.95 per book		$
Tennessee residents add $2.12 sales tax per book		$
Postage and handling at $3.00 per book		$
	TOTAL	$

Name _____

Address _____

City _____ State _____ Zip _____

Telephone _____

Method of Payment: [ ] American Express   [ ] Discover   [ ] MasterCard   [ ] VISA
                     [ ] Check payable to Peacock Hill Country Inn

Account Number _____ Expiration Date _____

Signature _____

Photocopies will be accepted.